Unfolding

My Wild & Precious Life

A Memoir of Transformation, Surrender & Joy

"*Unfolding My Wild & Precious Life* is more than a book. It's a carefully crafted guide to navigating some of life's deepest and most poignant human experiences. It is a beautiful blend of personal anecdotes, women's wisdom, and tangible tools to help any reader move through their own personal challenges. This book is a touching gift to anyone experiencing pain or loss of any kind. Anita so describes the difficult journey of infertility and loss as eloquently as she illustrates the often tricky dance between motherhood and career. It is a most heartful, touching handbook for life's hardest and most beautiful struggles."

~ Lianne Kim, Business Coach & Strategist | Founder & CEO of Mamas & Co.
www.liannekim.com | IG: @liannekimcoach

"Anita takes you on a journey of self-growth and discovery as she beautifully weaves in the tales of her own journey with the wisdom and insights she gained along the way. *Unfolding My Wild & Precious Life* is beautifully written and captures your attention from the first word to the last. Anita shares her vulnerability and in doing so will help so many other women. If you have ever felt alone on your journey or want help on how to upgrade your internal narrative, I highly recommend this book."

~ Julie Cass, Empowerment Coach | Founder of The Positive Change Group
www.thepositivechange.ca | IG: @thepositivechangegroup

"*Unfolding My Wild & Precious Life* is a thoughtfully written book, interwoven with valuable reminders that no matter how difficult our obstacles might seem in the moment, it is through our willingness to confront, embrace, and love the deepest, most authentic parts of ourselves that joy resides. It's a hopeful reminder of the beauty that awaits us in the lessons of life."

~ Brenda Vander Zanden, CEO | Course Creator & Consultant
www.brendaandco.ca | IG: @brendaandco.ca

"*Unfolding My Wild & Precious Life* allowed me to pause and reflect on where I can let go of fear and what I can make peace with in my life. As a professional working woman on my own motherhood journey, every chapter in this book resonated with me. If you're feeling alone in what you are going through, you will feel safe reading this book—and know that YOU matter."

~ Dr Abha Sharma, MD, Founder of Health Has No Finish Line | Writer | Podcaster www.
healthhasnofinishline.com | IG: _healthhasnofinishline

"*Unfolding My Wild & Precious Life* is the perfect combo of vulnerable storytelling and mindset coaching! I loved how Anita shared the depth of her experiences with me and then gave me, the reader, the opportunity in the moment of seeing how I could connect and apply action steps in my life. DOUBLE THE VALUE! The incredible power of storytelling in books like *Unfolding* is that it's a step toward dissolving harmful narratives around subjects like assisted fertility and unapologetically "choosing ourselves" as mothers and professionals. MORE OF THAT, PLEASE!"

~ Jake Lieske Willis, Motherhood Manifestation Mentor
www.thejaketake.com | IG: @jakeleiskewillis

"Reading this book feels like a warm, intimate conversation with your best friend. Anita's stories of love, loss, and learning deeply resonate, inspiring women to take tangible steps in claiming their authenticity and finding joy in a busy life."

- Carolyn Swora, MA I/O Psychology, Workplace Culture Architect and Leadership Coach
Best selling author of Rules of Engagement | IG: @carolynswora

Unfolding

My Wild & Precious Life

A MEMOIR OF TRANSFORMATION, SURRENDER & JOY

Anita Volikis

Table of Contents

"The Summer Day"
by Mary Oliver

Who made the world?

Who made the swan, and the black bear?

Who made the grasshopper?

This grasshopper, I mean—

the one who has flung herself out of the grass,

the one who is eating sugar out of my hand,

who is moving her jaws back and forth instead of up and down—

who is gazing around with her enormous and complicated eyes.

Now she lifts her pale forearms and thoroughly washes her face.

Now she snaps her wings open, and floats away.

I don't know exactly what a prayer is.

I do know how to pay attention, how to fall down

into the grass, how to kneel down in the grass,

how to be idle and blessed, how to stroll through the fields,

which is what I have been doing all day.

Tell me, what else should I have done?

Doesn't everything die at last, and too soon?

Tell me, what is it you plan to do

with your one wild and precious life?

Preface

It is December, and it is snowing. My five-year-old son is curled up beside me on the couch in our family room. His eyes are wide with wonder as he watches my fingers hit the keys of my laptop and the characters dance on the screen. His face radiates joy. He is transfixed by what he sees, fascinated by how quickly my fingers move. He touches my hand and asks, "How do you do that, Mommy?" and "Can I try?" I am overcome with love for this inquisitive, amazing little boy. He tells me he is going to spell his name. I wait patiently while he types the letters. As he hits the last key, he erupts into giggles.

"Look!" he says and points to the screen.

I smooth his hair and whisper into his ear, "Good for you. You did it!"

He looks up and frowns. "But I didn't do it as fast as you."

I smile. "Not yet, but you will one day." I kiss the top of his head, taking in the sweet scent of his hair, and I wish that time would stand still, for a little while anyway.

If you had told me ten years ago that I would be writing the manuscript of my book with my child curled up beside me, I probably would have laughed at you. I most certainly would not have believed you. I am a mother. I have a son. My heart is overflowing with love and gratitude for all that has happened in my life. Every experience. Every event. Every challenge. Every disappointment. Every loss. Every sorrow. Every failure. Every success. Every win. Every struggle. Every joy. For every moment that has nourished my unfolding.

Introduction

I have read Mary Oliver's poem "The Summer Day" so many times that it is indelible. The words are at once so relatable and incredibly profound. The line "Tell me, what is it you plan to do with your one wild and precious life" signifies a beautiful reminder to appreciate and cherish our ephemeral journey, *and to live.* The words are symbolic of my journey of leaning into challenge and change, learning to let go and surrender control, discovering and celebrating all my layers, and unfolding deeper into my self, my life, and my joy.

This book that you are holding in your hand or perhaps reading on a screen or listening to through a pair of earbuds has existed for a lot longer than its physical manifestation. It has been within me, inside of my heart, for years.

This book began as a tiny seed of a thought.

The tiny seed had long roots and a powerful vision. It was a vision of using my writing voice to share my experiences, to inspire self-transformation and reinvention, and to show you that you cannot get it wrong if you live from your highest self and trust in the power of the Universe to support you in manifesting what you truly desire.

The seed was nourished with water, earth, and intention. It soon grew a sprout and then a flower.

The vision grew, sustained by a powerful belief that I had a compelling voice and story to share, and by a persistent desire to accomplish what had been a long-held dream. The fantasy became something more, *something real.* Those moments of inspired but sporadic writing became a daily practice (well, most days anyway).

My dream became a passion and then a wonderful purpose. Before I knew it, I wrote the book that I wish I had read when I was navigating my own journey through marriage, infertility, motherhood, career change, creative pursuit, and, well, *life.*

Like most things that are worthwhile, writing this book had its share of challenges. Self-doubt and fear crept in every so often, particularly during the initial stages of my writing. I doubted that people would care to read my book, and I thought that even if they purchased it and read it, my story would ultimately fail to resonate and would disappoint. I feared judgment and criticism from my professional colleagues for daring to foray into such a personal exercise.

Most of all, I feared being perceived as self-indulgent in my choice to openly share parts of me that I have never shared before. When I was about two-thirds of the way through the manuscript, I happened upon the following about memoir writing by the immensely talented Sue Monk Kidd, one of my favorite fiction writers:

Writing memoir is gloriously self-indulgent and I'm perfectly okay with that. Women have been told so many times to be selfless that it can actually feel uncomfortable when we attempt to search for one.

When I write memoir, I'm undoubtedly in search of wholeness. Maybe I'm trying to resolve something, heal a wound, redeem some part of myself that has been orphaned or lost, or give a voice to what has been silenced. Maybe I'm trying to step into my truth. Maybe I'm trying to reveal myself to myself.

But here's something I didn't expect. Writing memoir can also be gloriously other-indulgent. The process not only takes me into myself, it frees me from myself. When I manage to distill my experience into meaning and integrate that meaning into my life through the creation of a narrative, I make it possible to move on without all the preoccupation and unconscious pull of the experience. It's the unexamined experience that wreaks the most havoc in my life and in my relationships.

The surprise is always this. The deeper we delve into our own lives, the more likely we are to tap into a universal experience. We find the portal to everyone.

These words have stayed with me.

While writing this book, I was immersed in a deeply personal unfolding and discovery of myself. However, the experience was about more than me. It was about connecting with the universal experiences of others, be they motherhood, infertility, professional transformation and reinvention, or creative pursuit. The eloquent words of Sue Monk Kidd reminded me that not only did I want to share my life experiences with others, *I needed to do so.* Her words reminded me that if I changed my mind and abandoned my writing, I would not only be short-changing myself, but I would also be depriving others of the opportunity to connect with a part of my journey and perhaps attain a pebble of insight, inspiration, or strength, or even simply the understanding that they are not alone. When I found this beautiful clarity, I returned to my writing with renewed excitement and purpose.

I experienced four transformations in my forties. Each of these involved a fundamental change to my self-image as well as emotional and spiritual growth that I never could have imagined. At forty-two, I became a mother after a long, complex, and remarkable fertility journey. At forty-six, I embarked upon a new career after nearly twenty years as a family lawyer. At forty-seven, I made the decision to share my creative spirit with the world and live my dream of writing and publishing my memoir. And at forty-eight, I returned to the practice of law, which has felt like coming full circle and equally like a new beginning because the act of resuming and re-embracing my profession has occurred at a different stage in my life and from my highest truest self. Some may call this a midlife identity crisis. I call it my unfolding, my awakening, and my embracing of who I have been all along: my authentic self.

We are multifaceted beings on a journey of unfolding and becoming that truly never ends. Life is a perpetual state of evolution. It doesn't wait for any of us. It keeps going, and if we allow ourselves to lean into challenges and embrace change, we, too, evolve along with it. Do I know what lies ahead on my life path? No. Is that okay? Absolutely.

Stories of resilience teach us that what matters is not so much the plan and roadmap to one's goals, but the growth and the alignment that occurs during the journey. Sharing our individual and collective experiences authentically and vulnerably is what makes us compassionate, empathetic beings. Our unique stories teach us that this rich, beautiful, complex, and chaotic journey we call "life" matters more than the ultimate destination.

My hope is that you, my reader, will find resonance within these pages. If you feel less alone and less afraid as a result of connecting with a chapter, a page, or even a few words, then I will know that sharing my book and leaning into my authenticity was worth the trials, the vulnerability, the rawness, and, ultimately, the joy and unparalleled experience of writing it.

Perhaps my book will ignite in you the courage to feel safe to tell yourself and those close to you that *all your experiences matter*, and to show you that change, reinvention, surrendering to peace, and letting go of fear, urgency, and struggle are all things that are part of your growth and that are *good*. As you read this book, I ask you to keep an open mind, to think beyond the four corners of your comfort zone, and to consider *the possibility* that there is more to living than the programming you were born with, that you grew up with, and that you have mastered. Allow yourself to consider that it is possible to navigate your life events and challenges by loosening the reins of control enough for a higher power—the Universe, God—to help you manifest what you truly desire. Allow yourself to consider that you are more than one thing. Allow yourself to consider "I am" as more than singular. I am, you are, multifaceted. I am, you are, many wonderful things. Finally, my hope is that you will feel ready to grow into and through your unique unfolding and to embrace what is rightfully and truly your destiny.

Chapter One

THE PLAN

I remember a time in my life when I started and ended my day in the depths of despair. This confession may sound like an exaggeration, but I assure you it is not. There is really no other way to describe it. The thick fog of heartache and sorrow would fill my head and engulf my heart as I tried to find sleep, quietly sobbing into my pillow so that I would not disturb my sleeping husband and remind him of the painful void plaguing our life. I would wake with the same all-consuming darkness saturating my thoughts and with a tiny word crushing my spirit and soul.

Why?

It is astounding how powerful a small word can be.

Why can't I be a mother?

Why can't I get pregnant?

Why can't I have a baby?

Why isn't this happening for me?

Why is this happening to me?

Why can't I have what I want?

Why?

Why?

Why?

From this state, I would move to autopilot: get showered and dressed, grab a quick breakfast (or not), and head out the door. On the drive to the office, I would usually stop at a Starbucks for a grande dark roast, thankful for the brief comfort of a hot beverage and the jolt of caffeine to prepare my mind for the focus it would need to begin the day's tasks. I would walk into my office, armor in place, eager to find solace in the seemingly endless responsibilities and challenges of being a lawyer.

A lawyer's day, specifically a family lawyer's day, is busy. In fact, *busy* is an understatement. There are client meetings to attend, phone calls to return, court material to draft, court attendances, phone meetings, emails, correspondence to draft, and continuing legal education materials to write (sometimes all in one day). The temporary distractions of a demanding law practice were plentiful, but inevitably, the fog would catch up. It would envelop me again, and I would shut my door, sit back in my chair, close my eyes, and relent to the onslaught of tears. Moments later, the phone would ring, or an email would arrive, and I would don the armor once more, along with plenty of problems and emergencies to distract me from my pain.

I hid it well—from my colleagues, friends, and some of my family. Even those who knew of my desire to have a child and had an idea of the efforts I had been making to get there were not aware of how profoundly my wish to be a mother was affecting my daily life. On the surface, I was a busy, positive, upbeat, and successful lawyer who was well-liked by her clients and peers, a happily married woman who had a loving husband, a solid marriage, a beautiful home, and a life for which to be thankful.

Underneath it all, I was falling apart.

I also remember a time several years later when I would begin and end my day with a clearer mind and an open heart, my heartache and anguish replaced by lightness, peace, and gratitude. It was a deep gratitude for my health, my husband, our dog, our home, our family and friends, my career, and ultimately, gratitude for our child. The fog had finally lifted, cleared, and made way for the warming rays of sunshine and infinite limitless sky.

I gave birth to my son, my only child, at age forty-two. I hadn't envisioned becoming a mother in my forties. That wasn't *part of the plan*. But then again, I never expected that I would experience infertility, miscarry twice, and navigate assisted reproduction and adoption before conceiving naturally and giving birth. At forty-two. None of these things were "part of the plan."

The "plan" was a straight line: go to university, get an undergraduate degree and a law degree, begin my legal career, become successful, meet and marry my "soul mate," become a mother, and live happily ever after. Really, in that order and preferably by my early thirties. I thrived on order. Ducks in a row? I had flocks of them in rows and rows. Spontaneity did not factor into my life plan. I didn't really care for surprises. I thought and researched meticulously and then executed with focus and determination. This strategy worked for a lot of things. But it did not work for everything.

Life is not meant to be linear. It is also not meant to be predictable. Life is a bright, colorful canvas. It is a dance of dips and twirls, and missteps, and leaps, and falls. I now understand that life is a harmony of scripted storyline and tangential tales. I believe that a life well lived is less choreography and more improvisation.

This is what makes life rich and memorable. This is what makes it interesting and exciting. *This is what makes life worth living.* This lesson was taught to me in a number of powerful and beautiful ways.

I am not the same person I was twenty-five years ago. That person, the twenty-something-year-old, was idealistic and somewhat naïve. She tended to see things as black or white, right or wrong, easy or difficult, possible or impossible. She dreamed, she planned, she took action. And if she did each of these things well, she inevitably succeeded and got what she wanted. Not a *bad* outlook or work ethic, truth be told, but one that was somewhat of a fallacy.

In my thirties and forties, I came to understand that, as author Michael A. Singer says, *"most of life will unfold in accordance with forces far outside your control, regardless of what your mind says about it."* The sooner you accept this truth, the more you will appreciate and enjoy the journey. Recognizing that there are forces outside of you—the Universe, God, whatever you wish to label them—and relinquishing control is freeing. Surrendering is beautifully freeing.

Loosening the reins of control and leaning into trust does not mean being a passive participant in your life. You can surrender while being an active full participant in your journey. We all have the capability to be at cause, to be the creators of our lives and futures. Notwithstanding the challenges and obstacles we encounter, we have the ability to mold our thoughts, shape our actions, and create our results, even in the face of the unpredictable, the difficult, the seemingly impossible. That is growth. Now, if we are living in effect, rather than cause, we become the passive and powerless recipients of life's impediments and blows, and ultimately, resentful and unhappy victims of circumstance rather than conscious creators of our destinies.

How many of us say we are "living" but are truly missing the forest for the trees? How many of us are settling for the destination at the expense of the adventure? Is this truly living? Shouldn't we be extracting as much growth and joy from the journey rather than making it a means to an end?

As I navigated my own life challenges in my thirties and forties, I came to learn that it is possible to *over* plan. I began to understand that planning is really a double-edged sword. Planning places the focus on arriving, on that point in the distant future rather than on the unfolding of the journey, *now*, and *on living*. I am grateful that I developed the awareness that in chronically planning and preparing for the life I thought I needed, I was losing sight of the precious and also fleeting journey. I also understood that my plan had been getting in the way of a much larger plan, the Universe's plan for me, *when and in the way that it was intended for me.*

Pause, reflect, lean in

- *Are you a planner?*
- *Where in your life do you find yourself over planning?*
- *Can you remember what it was like when you did not plan something and ventured "off the path?"*
- *Can you remember the last time you allowed yourself to freefall into joy, surprise, and the wonders of the present?*
- *How did it feel to let go?*
- *In what area of your life are you prepared to let go and loosen the reins of control?*

Chapter Two

Roots and Wings

There are only two lasting bequests we can hope to give our children.
One of these is roots, the other, wings.

–Hodding Carter

My upbringing is best described with one word: love. I was incredibly fortunate to have two wonderful, devoted, loving parents. Both of Greek descent, they immigrated to Canada from the island of Imbros, Turkey, in the late sixties and early seventies. If you have not heard of Imbros, you are certainly not alone. Not many know of this beautiful and historically significant island. Imbros is one of two islands (the second being Tenedos) in the North Aegean that form the western entrance to the Dardanelles, the internationally significant waterway forming part of the continental boundary between Europe and Asia. Hearing my parents describe their birthplace left me imagining a rustic, natural land where its inhabitants lived simple lives of mostly farmers. My parents liked to recount that they lived in the same community and the families knew each other, although my parents did not really spend time together. I was always fascinated by this information; my parents grew up in the same village, in the same neighborhood, and later married each other. Wow.

My father immigrated to Toronto, Canada, in 1969 at the age of twenty-three. His parents and three of his four siblings had moved to Canada before he did. My father did not know how to speak English. He spoke Greek. In 1971, my mother, at twenty-one years of age, also immigrated to Toronto. She left her family to move to a country that was entirely foreign to her in every sense of the word. She also did not know the language.

I often think about what that must have been like for my parents. My father moved to a country on the other side of the world, to a large city, where he did not know the language or culture. My mother lived her teenage years away from her family for much of the year, living with and working for an affluent family in a cosmopolitan city that was unlike anything she had ever experienced. After my father proposed to her through correspondence, she moved again to the other side of the world—to a country where she did not have a single relative. This move must have been a tremendous change for them. They were married in 1971, and I was born in 1973. My sister and brother followed, in 1975 and 1978.

My Greek culture was prominent in my upbringing. My first words were spoken in Greek because that is how my parents communicated with me and with each other. We essentially learned the

English language together. I recently told my son that I learned to speak English by watching *Sesame Street*. By the time I entered junior kindergarten, I was fluent in English; however, when I was emotional or upset about something, I would often revert to my first language.

Our family followed the customs and traditions of Greek culture and practiced Greek Orthodoxy, part of the Eastern Orthodox Christian faith. My parents were religious in the sense that they respected and followed their religious upbringing, married in the Greek Orthodox Church, followed its rituals and traditions, and raised us with the values of the Church. However, they were also independent thinkers, particularly my mother who was not afraid to question and voice her opinion about religion, politics, and just about anything. I am very much like my mother in this way.

My father is a quiet and humble man. He always worked extremely hard—and not once did I hear him complain about it. He was diligent, working factory jobs for most of his life. He was also a very devoted husband and father. His self-image was that of a provider, and his paramount concern was the well-being of his family. My mother raised three children and was the most incredible nurturer. She stayed home with us for almost all my childhood. The words "hard-working," "humble," and "devoted provider" describe my father. The words "loving," "self-less," "strong," and "of the highest integrity" describe my mother.

I have always had a close relationship with each of my parents, but in different ways. I adored my father as I was growing up and knew how to talk him into getting what I wanted. My dad taught me diligence, patience, calmness, and what it meant to have a strong work ethic. He taught me how to ride my metallic orange-and-black "pacer deluxe" two-wheeler when I was six or seven years old. He patiently walked up and down the street for what must have felt like hours, lightly holding the metal handle on the back of the banana seat (pretending he wasn't when I noticed) and then letting go but staying very near to make sure I was okay and comforting me but also encouraging me to get back on the bike when I fell down. I could always count on my dad to drive me where I needed to go, to pick me up from my part-time job, and to walk the two blocks from our home to meet me at the bus stop after my late evening university classes to accompany me home. Dad took my siblings and me ice skating at the Scarborough Civic Center most winter weekends, where we skated for hours and then sipped hot chocolate before returning to a wonderful meal that our mother had prepared. He took us to and from our Greek school lessons on Saturday mornings. And he helped me with my math homework and showed me that long division was not something to fear. He taught me to approach problems with patience and to find joy in simplicity.

My mother was the parent I was closest to—my nurturer, my protector, and truly, my hero. She was the person who had the greatest effect on my life. I shared things with her that most would only share with a closest friend. She was the parent and the woman I aspired to be. I admired her strength and integrity. She taught me to live authentically and to be true to myself. She taught me that my self-worth mattered more than others' opinions. My mother passed away while I was writing this book. She lives in my heart and soul every day.

The thought of my mother will always evoke unwavering love. She loved me when I was a tenacious, curious child. She loved me when I was bullied at school as an adolescent. She loved me when I was a teenager with an answer for everything. She loved me and dried my tears after I broke up with my first boyfriend. She loved me when I sought my independence in my twenties as a law student. She loved me when I cried about the demands of my job as a new lawyer. She loved me when I suffered two miscarriages, despite not relating to what I was experiencing. She loved me through the challenges of assisted reproduction, something that was entirely unknown to her. She loved me when I grieved the sudden death of my in-laws and when she became a second mother to my husband. She loved me when I became a mother and experienced the highs and lows of a first-time parent. She loved me when I had a breast lumpectomy and radiation treatment in the months before she passed. But my mother could not love me and comfort me as I lived through the most painful experience of my lifetime, her final days in and departure from this world. I lived this heartbreak soon after I began writing this book—a book that she encouraged me to write and share with the world.

My parents taught me the importance of family, loyalty, determination, humility, freedom, and gratitude. Their stories of growing up in a village have always filled me with pride and admiration. Their lives were not easy. They were born in the forties in a part of the world where struggle shaped the experiences of its inhabitants. Imbros's significant Greek population was greatly reduced due to forced expulsions by the Turkish government. My parents were able to speak their language, follow their customs and culture, and practice their Christian faith (Greek Orthodoxy), but their lives were heavily influenced by their Turkish government. Their school curriculum required them to learn the Turkish language and culture in addition to their Greek language, culture, and other studies. Each of my parents grew up in large families to parents who farmed. I marveled at learning that my father apprenticed with a tailor when he was a teenager and that *at age thirteen*, my mother began working as an au pair for a Jewish family in Istanbul where she, still very much a child herself, was responsible for caring for two children. *She was thirteen.* She would return home to her family several times a year, primarily during holidays and special occasions. I understand that my mother grew up at a time when families had unique challenges and when children had to grow up a lot earlier than they do in the world that I was born into. But a part of me has never been able to understand this part of my mother's experience and, in many ways, found it unimaginable.

My mother spoke with me at length about her experience living with and working for that family in Istanbul. When she shared her memories, she did so with joy but also with nostalgia and sadness for her young childhood and the loss she felt having lived almost the entirety of her teenage years away from her family. Although I could not possibly relate, hearing my mother's words made me admire her strength and resilience. I marveled at the life my mother lived that was so different from mine.

I remember my childhood, adolescence, and young adulthood as joyful. I had two wonderful parents and two amazing siblings. I lived in a home where I felt safe, cared for, free, welcomed, loved and nurtured, which does not mean that everything came easily and that my family life was without its challenges. Of course, we had challenges, financial and otherwise, but the love was always there and that is what is deeply ingrained in my memory. To this day, when I think of my family, I feel love.

I was fortunate to share my childhood with a younger sister and brother. We have always been very close in our relationship. Like most siblings, we got on each other's nerves, argued, and drove our parents crazy at times. But we loved and looked out for one another. We were siblings but also friends in many ways, which was especially the case between my sister and me, as we grew up closely together. My first words to my sister following her birth were something to the effect of "What is this thing doing in my bed?" Two-year-old me had just transitioned from my crib to a bed, and I was astounded to see someone else in *my* crib. I eventually adjusted to no longer being the only child. When I learned that my mom was expecting a third child and that I was going to have another sibling, I was overjoyed. And when our baby brother was born, I was ecstatic. When my sister and I met our brother for the first time, my exclamation of "Mom, I'm so proud of you" stunned my parents. I was five. My sister and I shared a bedroom until I moved out to begin law school. We envied our brother for having his own room, but truth be told, I didn't really mind sharing my space with my sister; I came to cherish the late-night whispers and giggles and her quiet and comforting snores in the night.

My parents and siblings and the love and nurturing that I received growing up made me feel secure and unconditionally loved throughout my youth and into my adulthood. It truly was my grounding, and for that, I am eternally grateful.

Pause, reflect, lean in

- *How would you describe your familial roots? What role do you believe they have played in your journey to and through adulthood to the present time?*

- *Not everyone has experienced a loving, emotionally nurturing childhood. I realize that for some, childhood memories are triggering and even painful. But our families are not defined by biology and DNA. For you, family may signify closely bonded friendships, people who have supported you and held space for you outside of the nuclear or traditional family.*

- *How have those who represent "family" to you affected your life, and what imprint have they made along your journey?*

Chapter Three

THE TALKER, THE SINGER, THE PERFORMER, THE ACHIEVER

When I was three, my parents nicknamed me "the little lawyer." Can you guess why? *I would not stop talking.* I was able to articulate what I wanted and how I felt from a very young age. I also lacked a filter for what was appropriate behavior. Apparently, when we had guests over and it started getting dark, I would tell them to "get going home now, it's almost your bedtime." Beneath their nervous laughter, my parents were quietly mortified. As a young child, I was quite animated when I spoke and had a flair for drama. I had an answer for everything (in both English and Greek), and I *always* had to have the last word.

I was an inquisitive and tenacious five-year-old when I met "Santa Claus" *in my home.* Santa was not visiting during the night when all the children were asleep in their beds with "visions of sugar plums dancing in their heads." It was an impromptu meet-and-greet. Santa stopped by shortly before my bedtime with his great big bag full of gifts. Well, I took a close look at "Santa" once he walked *through our door* (the first sign that something was amiss) with a red suit, beard, and all, and I recognized him for who he truly was: our neighbor from four houses down the street. My suspicions began before I even got a good look at him. He had, after all, knocked on our door. He didn't slide down the chimney. When my mother saw the look of recognition cross my face, she cautioned me with a finger to her lips so that I would not spoil the surprise for my sister (our infant brother was already asleep and oblivious to the commotion) who was very excited about meeting Santa Claus. You should have seen the look of dread followed by relief wash over "Santa's" face when he realized that I had figured out who he was, but I was not going to "spill the beans" after all, or at least not as long as my mother remained in the room. You might think that I was disappointed or angry that it was an impostor posing as Santa stopping by our home. But I was so busy being proud of the fact that I had figured out the culprit's identity and keeping the secret from my little sister to care about being duped by my parents and our neighbor.

Growing up, I was a high-achiever and believed that I had to excel at everything. This belief was not the product of parental influence or pressure. My parents were my biggest supporters, ingraining in my mind that I was enough and that doing my best is what mattered. The pressure that I was experiencing was all self-created. However, I was young and still had a lot of growing up to do.

When I first learned that I would have the opportunity to play a musical instrument in grade four, I was *thrilled*. I wanted to play the violin, but because there were no string instruments at my school, I chose the clarinet. From the moment I picked up the instrument and touched its chrome keys, I was in love. I joined the school band and continued performing in school bands and orchestras throughout elementary, middle school, and high school. I practiced several times a week (weekends too), sitting on the edge of my bed and using my desk chair as a music stand. I loved playing. When my siblings started playing musical instruments, we would sometimes practice together. I can't say that the sounds in our house were particularly pleasing on those days that we happened to be playing at the same time (have you heard a clarinet, trombone, and trumpet playing at the same time but not following the same piece of music?), but it gave my parents tremendous joy to hear us "making music" together. It gave us great joy as well.

I loved to sing. I sang in choirs throughout school. I loved expanding my vocal range, taking my ability to new levels and experiencing my voice mature and develop intensity. I enjoyed performing. The feeling of butterflies was welcomed and made me even more excited to give it my all. Singing gave me so much joy. I truly believe that pursuing an activity in the arts such as musical performance does wonders for a child's self-esteem.

In the summer after my eighth birthday, my family moved to Scarborough from East York, Toronto. It was my first year at my new school, and I was in grade three. I had made a few friends—children from my neighborhood—that past summer, but I was quite nervous about joining a new school and meeting new classmates and a new teacher. Our class was instructed to choose a poem or short story and recite it to the class. I chose to do something a little different; I chose to sing a song. I gave an animated performance of "There Was an Old Lady Who Swallowed a Fly," a song that I had learned the year before at my previous school. For those of you who are not familiar with it, it's a long one and the lyrics tend to be morbid. Apparently, it was not a familiar song to my classmates and our teacher who were really surprised and entertained by my rendition. I made such an impression that my teacher had me perform it during the school's regular Speech Arts' Festival.

I spent the rest of elementary school and middle school regularly performing in front of audiences. It was a lot of fun and helped my self-confidence. I auditioned for and got the lead in the Pinocchio musical in grade six. I was so excited. I think I may still have the script I used to recite my lines. I recently shared photographs of the performance with my son who was fascinated to learn that his mother played the role of *a boy* whose nose grew because he lied. However, it was during middle school that I really grew into my passion for singing and performing. My most memorable of these experiences was singing Whitney Houston songs for our school talent shows and really learning to be comfortable in front of an audience. It was great fun.

In high school, I was fortunate to have an remarkable choirmaster who was a trained opera singer. Learning from such a huge talent was an unforgettable experience. During our first rehearsal when I joined the choir in grade nine, when I proceeded to take my place among the altos, she asked me to sing a couple of verses of a song, and when I was done, she told me that I was welcome to sing alto but that I was most definitely a soprano. I was perplexed. I had always thought of myself as an alto, but she had other plans for me. I spent the next while developing that range of my singing and demonstrating to those who heard me sing and, more importantly, to myself, that I was indeed a soprano. Singing brought me tremendous joy and cultivated my self-confidence.

During my first musical theater production in grade nine, I belted out a solo (in the role of a young Viking) with a great deal of passion and had members of the audience approaching me at the conclusion of the performance to congratulate me and encourage me to pursue a career in musical theater. You can imagine what this praise did for my self-image as a new high school student. I participated in musical theater productions throughout those years, the most memorable of which was filled with the music of Rodgers and Hammerstein and Leonard Bernstein. Performing "I Feel Pretty" at the then Royal York Hotel (now Fairmont Royal York) in Toronto is one of my fondest memories.

Writing speeches and delivering them was something I enjoyed doing as a child and teenager. I loved the creative process of writing and was equally excited to give a presentation. I practiced and practiced. I would often stand in front of the large mirror above the dresser in my bedroom and "perform" this way. It was fun. I got nervous, but the feeling of butterflies only reinforced that I was doing something I was excited about, not something I feared. One of my greatest memories was having the incredible honor of introducing the Honorable Lincoln Alexander, Lieutenant Governor of Ontario, to my middle school during a Remembrance Day program. I was in grade eight and about thirteen years old. There were other esteemed guests in attendance, including William Davis, the MPP of our riding. I wrote a speech, recited it several times, had my cue cards ready, and was incredibly excited (and quite nervous) about the event. As I was walking to the podium, I realized that I had left my cards somewhere else. But I pressed on and soon realized that I didn't really need them. Later, in the staff room, Mr. Davis told me that he wished he spoke half as well and was half as poised as I was when addressing an audience. Those words stayed with me for a long time.

Little did I realize then just how much these interests, passions, and experiences would influence who I would become as I grew older. Little did I know that these would be the very tools that would help me rediscover my true self, my authentic core beneath the pressures and demands of adulthood. Looking back at these memories has reminded me that I am a woman of many interests and talents. It has reminded me that I can lean into these pieces of myself, including my creative self—a part of me that I have dimmed during my adulthood—and apply them to how I navigate my personal and professional life. I thought about my younger self and the excitement she felt when she was performing that solo, reciting those lines, or addressing an audience as I prepared for a meeting or court hearing, as I wrote my book, or as I guided my son through a new activity. The experiences are there, ready for me to lean into and embrace.

Pause, reflect, lean in 

- *What is something you loved to do as a child?*

- *Have you returned to that interest or activity in adulthood? If so, how did it make you feel? If you haven't, what stopped you?*

- *Does a particular childhood experience or event stand out in your memory? How has it affected you and shaped your adult self?*

- *Do you ever lean into a fond memory from childhood—perhaps a memory when you were performing or playing a beloved sport—when you're navigating life's challenges?*

- *If you had the opportunity, what is something you would tell your ten-year-old self?*

- *What is something you would tell your teenage self? What would you say to your twenty-something self?*

- *Who do you believe you are at your authentic core? Do you see a resonance of your younger self there?*

Chapter Four

"SOLUTIONS, NOT PROBLEMS"

I have exceptionally vivid memories of my elementary and middle school years. Among these memories are those of my teachers. I had many teachers who I greatly admired and who I credit with having encouraged me as I pursued my talents and interests. However, less than a handful of teachers truly stand out as having had a profound impact on how I view the world. One such teacher was my grade eight homeroom teacher.

My introduction to mantras and affirmations occurred at a young age. My grade eight homeroom teacher, a kind, patient, and wise man (and one of the best teachers I have ever had), created a mantra for the class. I don't believe he called it a mantra, but that is the word I'm using to describe it. The words "Solutions, Not Problems" were written on the chalkboard every morning and slowly became tattooed on our minds and, as I came to realize many years later, in my subconscious.

We started each day with a journaling practice, and this phrase was one of our writing prompts. I really enjoyed the exercise and loved writing in my journal. I remember getting home from school on the day that this class activity was introduced and excitedly sharing the news with my mother. Well, my mother thought it was the most amazing thing in the world. "Solutions, not problems" soon became *our family* mantra that stuck for probably the next ten years. Who am I kidding? It has never unstuck.

When I had an argument with my sister about which part of the closet was hers and which was mine or I complained about a calculus test that I did not feel good about or an argument that I had with my best friend, my mother would wrap me in her embrace and look into my eyes and say, "Solutions, not problems." Then we would take a few minutes to discuss what had happened and ways that we could improve the situation or rise from it.

We did this routine a lot.
Actually, we did it all of the time.
All. Of. The. Time.

It started to become a little tiresome. I remember rolling my eyes when I heard my mother use the sing-songy phrase, "Solutions, not problems, Anthoula." She would almost always call me by my Greek name, the name I was given at birth, throughout my childhood. Did she ever love using the phrase! And did I ever start regretting sharing it with her! To be honest, it wasn't so bad. After a period of time of disliking the phrase and cringing at the sound of it, the words started to grow on me again as I got older.

SOLUTIONS, NOT PROBLEMS.

That simple phrase taught me that wherever there was a problem, a solution existed nearby. It reminded me to take a breath, to pause, to exhale, and to assess what was happening from a different perspective. It taught me to remove myself from the murkiness of the situation that was troubling me, to step outside of it, and to look within myself with the comfort and love of my mother by my side. The phrase was a self-confidence mantra. It was a reminder that the key—the solution to whatever was troubling me, whatever seemed unsolvable—lay deep within me. All I had to do was trust myself to uncover the solution and wisdom that was already there.

Over time, I developed a deeper understanding of these words. Problems, troubles, difficulties exist. They are inevitable. They are a fact of life. The goal is to prevent them from taking over our lives. The key is to use your energy not dwelling on the problem but focusing on finding the solution, a solution that is likely right there in front of you but that you cannot yet see. That is the goal.

In more recent years, the phrase that I use has evolved to "Seek out solutions, do not dwell in the land of problems." Here is my current summary of what this phrase means to me:

You cannot solve a problem from the same wavelength or frequency of that problem.

You need awareness to solve a problem.

To gain that awareness, you need to distance and detach yourself from the problem.

To solve the problem, you must get on the frequency of the solution.

Do you remember a time when you experienced an "aha moment?"

I'm sure you can remember when you were exhausted from all of the time, effort, and money you invested in resolving an issue or undertaking a task, only to abandon it out of sheer overwhelm. Then, out of the blue, the answer magically appeared before your eyes, the solution falling into your lap.

I have news for you.

The solution did not miraculously or magically appear, the answer didn't suddenly fall into your lap.

It was always there.

It's true. It was always there. But you were not ready to see it. You were not aligned with it. You were so caught up in the struggle and the strife that the answer passed you by. It was only after you removed yourself from the struggle and the strife and you changed course that you were able to see the solution and align with it.

By changing the frequency we are on, much like we change the tuning dial on an analog radio (you know, the one where you need to move the dial oh so carefully and then voilà! static transforms to clear, crisp sound), we align with the answer, the solution, the result that we desire. Think of a time in your life when you changed your frequency, then reaped the rewards.

I have started using the phrase—"There is a solution to every problem"—when I am interacting with my son, and he doesn't seem to mind it. And since he doesn't seem to mind it, I am running with it.

A couple of months ago, my son was having trouble reading a word in a chapter book that is much too advanced for him. He frowned, slammed the book shut, and declared that the book was "not suitable" (a new favorite phrase), and he wouldn't be reading it anymore. I took his hands in mine, looked at him, and said, "There is always a solution to every problem." I wasn't sure that he understood, but he did stop complaining about the book and seemed a lot less upset. Then another day, when he was getting frustrated building something out of Lego, I began reciting, "Remember, there is a solution to—" "every problem," he completed for me, his mouth forming into a smile. Well, that was certainly a proud mom moment.

Pause, reflect, lean in

- *When you are struggling with something, what is the story you tell yourself? Is it a compassionate story or is it a critical one?*

- *What is a problem you are currently facing?*

- *How much of the problem is coming from an external force and how much of it is created by your own thoughts and beliefs?*

- *How would it feel to change frequencies, to lean in, and to allow the answer to surface?*

- *Are you willing to be open to the answer and to tell yourself that it already exists within you? Are you willing to receive it?*

Chapter Five

What Do You Want to Be When You Grow Up?

What is likely the most asked question of a child?

"What do you want to be when you grow up?"

Agreed? All right, then.

Family members, teachers, friends—just about everyone I knew asked me this question numerous times throughout my childhood and adolescence. I'm sure I'm not alone here and that if you and I are of the same generation, then *you*, too, were asked this question. I used to love answering it. I enjoyed formulating an answer that made me excited about my future, and one that impressed the person posing the question and met their expectations of me. As an adult, I came to appreciate the value of asking a child this type of question. It would encourage them to have dreams and goals to aspire to and to use their imagination. I wouldn't realize until much later just how deeply rooted in societal expectations this line of questioning was. It felt like a permission slip. If I answered "correctly," meaning if the person asking the question was impressed by my answer, it felt like validation, permission, a hall pass to go be/do/have exactly what my answer was. I see that now, in hindsight. More recently, I have realized that the phrase is quite problematic. To some degree, it is constraining. While it may be a wonderful thing for a child of eight or nine or ten to use their imagination about their life ahead and the possibilities that await them, why does a high school student need to "decide" what they want to be? Why can't they use their imagination and feel free to think in a nonlinear way—to feel that they can think about ways in which they would like to live their lives, the characteristics they want to embody as a contributing member of society, the interests they want to pursue rather than a linear path to a single job or career?

I am not, for one moment, suggesting that we do away with the question and expunge it from our interactions with children and youth. I do not have a problem with the phrase itself and with asking our children and youth to use their imagination and to consider possibilities for their future. What I have a problem with is the perhaps unintended expectations that we instill in children and youth to make an ultimate decision about their future and the reinforcing of a linear path of growth that I now understand is fundamentally flawed. What

I have a problem with is the implication that achievement and success means deciding on a single path and pursuing it vigorously without veering away from that distant goal. What I have a problem with is valuing traditional educational paths at the expense of interests, talents, and fiery passions. Why can't we merge both? Why can't both paths be explored?

Why can't the question be **"What kind of person do you want to be when you grow up?"** thus encouraging our children and youth to think about values and characteristics? "I want to be loving," "I want to help people," "I want people to respect me," "I want to be loved," "I want to have friends," "I want to be happy," "I want to spread joy."

Can you imagine the society we would be creating if we shifted the focus away from a "job" and "career" and "degree" and toward a way of conducting one's life? Imagine for one moment the incredible ripple effect it would create.

I was raised at a time when education and career paths followed a more traditional trajectory. You went to school, got a degree, and attained a job in the field for which you had trained. I always enjoyed school from a very young age. And I followed a linear path through my education and career—until more recently anyway.

My memories of "what I want to be when I grow up" are exceptionally vivid. Like most children, my dreams vacillated between several options, some fictional, some real. Here they are in the order I can best recall them.

Wonder Woman at age five. I spent a lot of time spinning around my living room, bedroom, and backyard, trying to lasso my toys ("bad guys") and even my sister with my jump rope to make them tell the truth. It was epic! I felt invincible, bold, and very much like Wonder Woman, who could make anything happen!

Kelly Garrett, one of the infamous Charlie's Angels, at age six. I had a huge crush on Kelly. She was my idol. I wanted to look like her, act like her, *be her.* We had a neighbor two houses away who I decided to name Kelly because she had hair like her. Come to think of it, their hair was probably the only characteristic they shared. I was basically "Kelly's" mini stalker for an entire summer, appearing at her front door or venturing into her backyard for an opportunity to talk to her or shyly look at her and smile. She thought it was cute. I now think it was weird but also a little cute.

Teacher at age seven. I loved school and admired my teachers. I was also a little bit afraid of some of my teachers who appeared to wield a certain amount of control over their classrooms. I looked up to my teachers, and I wanted others to look at me the same way. I wanted to mentor the way they did. They emanated influence, and even when I was seven, I sensed just how powerful that could be when used in integrity.

Paleontologist at age eight. When I first learned about dinosaurs, I was transfixed. When I first visited the Royal Ontario Museum (ROM) on a school trip and saw all those gigantic bones, I was in awe. I may not have known the term "paleontologist" at the time, but I was interested in working with dinosaur bones and learning more about these amazing creatures. There was mystery and beauty within the relics of the past. These once-gigantic creatures ruled the Earth. I felt like we were in a silent reverie at the ROM, paying homage to the magnificence that once was while embracing our own evolution.

Veterinarian at age nine or ten. I have always loved animals and had a strong desire to help them. I thought vets were heroes (and they truly are). When I realized that vets also had to tend to ill animals, some of whom they could not help, I realized that being a veterinarian was not the job for me.

Orchestra conductor at age eleven. What can I say? Music. And the conductor seemed to have quite a bit of power. He or she *made* music. How incredible is it to move synchronously with your fellow choir or orchestra members? There was and is power in synergy and cooperation.

Singer at age eleven or twelve. Well, also music! Imagine a job where I could sing, write songs, create music, and perform all day? How fun!

Lawyer at age twelve or thirteen. This choice was bound to happen. I was a talker and a performer (did I mention I could be very dramatic?). I also loved to argue.

Criminal lawyer at ages fourteen through sixteen. Television was my influence here. But I also wanted to make the world a safer place, and I thought practicing criminal law was a way to do it.

Politician at age seventeen or eighteen. The news, influence, power, and the ability to shape government and society. Wow.

Supreme Court Justice at age eighteen. I would practice law, become a judge, and eventually be appointed to the highest court in Canada. Easy-peasy.

Crown Attorney at ages nineteen through twenty-one. Obtaining justice for victims. Hmm. Upholding *the law*. Punishing those who broke the law. Wielding justice. Powerful.

Constitutional/human rights lawyer at ages twenty-two through twenty-seven. Equality for all. Feminism. Opportunity. Human rights. When I studied the Canadian Charter of Rights and Freedoms, I was enthralled.

I never imagined becoming a family lawyer.

I saw the movie *Kramer vs. Kramer* as a teenager, and although the courtroom scenes intrigued me, I did not relish the idea of fighting about a child. Truth be told, it made me very uncomfortable. I took two family law courses in law school and found them interesting. Did I want to practice family law at that point? Well, no. But I thought it was a decent "plan B" in case the constitutional/human rights lawyer path didn't pan out for me.

I decided I wanted to become a lawyer when I was about thirteen—a time when my mind should have been on more "age appropriate" ideas, like when my next outing to the mall with friends would be and whether so and so was into me as much as I was into him. Yep. And in case you're wondering, my parents had nothing to do with it. Becoming a lawyer was my idea and decision alone.

There were no lawyers in my family, and the only thing I knew about lawyers at that time came from watching a few *Perry Mason* episodes and the occasional courtroom scene on prime-time television. Then, in my later teenage years when I discovered *Law & Order*, I was more than intrigued. I was hypnotized by the drama, the power, and the incredibly interesting lives these people lived each day. I was hooked. I was set on becoming a "prosecutor" or "crown attorney," to mete out justice and make society a safer place. I could not imagine defending someone who was guilty. Lawyers looked powerful, delivered justice, and their jobs were exciting and prestigious. Lawyers knew how to grab people's attention, persuade with their words, and captivate an audience, all of which drew me in. I had no concept of the hours they worked or of the lifestyles they lived or of the money they could earn. None of that crossed my mind. It was my perceived importance of their role, the ability to "make a difference" in the world and "keep society safe" that attracted me to the profession.

With the decision to become a lawyer came a desire for a plan to get there. I remember meeting with my high school guidance counselor in grade nine and announcing that I wanted to be a lawyer and that I needed "guidance" to do it. I knew that excelling academically was key, but I wanted to know the courses I should take in the balance of high school and university to prepare me and increase my chances of getting accepted to law school. My guidance counselor smiled, praised me for my determination, then proceeded to explain, gently, that I had years ahead of me, and although it was wonderful that I was thinking about my future, I should keep an open mind, as I was bound to change it a few times. I don't think I was really listening to her by that point.

During my undergraduate degree, I was methodical about the courses I took. I completed a major in political science and a minor in French. I had developed an interest in Canadian politics from one of my courses in high school, and I had always excelled in and enjoyed French. Since I wanted to attain the grade point average to increase my chances of being accepted to law school, focusing my undergraduate degree in these areas made sense. I took courses in Canadian politics and political theory and became so interested in the latter that I briefly considered a career in academia—briefly because, well, the plan was law school. My French courses were wonderful, particularly those in French linguistics. In my first year of my three-year undergraduate degree, I took sociology and psychology and became passionate about those studies. I also briefly considered pursuing psychology; it was the most enjoyable of my first-year courses. These were also brief considerations because they did not fit into my plan.

I enjoyed my university experience, learned from amazing professors, met wonderful friends, and excelled. But the choices I made, my experiences, my academic and social life, were all restricted by my plan. I had a part-time job, working a few hours a week at retail stores between grade ten and my final year of my undergraduate degree so that I could purchase my textbooks and have my own spending money. Between my studies and my part-time job, there was little time for anything else. My ultimate goal was to achieve the marks to be accepted to law school. I knew it was competitive and that I had to work harder than ever. Unfortunately, the admirable work ethic I developed by that time came at the expense of continuing a pursuit of music (a constant in my life until then) because I deemed it to be too distracting in the pursuit of my ultimate goal.

Music had been a *huge* part of my life. In fact, just about every happy memory of my school years was connected to music in some way. I remember my grade seven and eight music teacher's surprise and disappointment when I conveyed that I wanted to be a lawyer. I believe his words to me were something to the effect of "Are you sure? Do you really want to settle for that when you have such musical talent, such a gift?" What I naïvely believed at the time but was embarrassed to express to my teacher (or to anyone) was that pursuing music would mean that my academic achievements would have been for naught. That I would, in fact, be settling if I "gave up" the chance of a career that was built on the foundation of my academic accomplishments and pursued one that was founded in music, which was something I viewed as secondary to academics. Music was something that I was good at and loved, but I did not see it as the foundation on which to build my future.

I own a clarinet. It was a birthday present from my parents when I turned twenty or so, and I was thrilled and extremely touched to receive it. The decision to give me a clarinet came from what my parents saw had been missing from my life. When I stopped playing in a school orchestra, I lost the ability to use a musical instrument that was provided by the school. I did not own my own clarinet, so the gift from my parents was truly amazing. I did play it once in a while when the mood struck me. But I am ashamed to say that it had been nearly ten years since I opened the case when I took it out of the closet this past year. I was afraid I wouldn't remember how to play. I guess it's like riding a bike; it comes back to you, quickly. I surprised myself by playing a few notes and avoiding squeaks (Dylan, my golden retriever, was also thankful). I was afraid to look for some sheet music and give it a go. I wasn't able to go that far; maybe next time. Playing the clarinet hasn't been the only thing I've missed. Aside from singing to my son (and sometimes in the shower or while driving), I have not done any serious singing, and I can tell that my voice and range have suffered. You have to use it, right? Your voice is bound to change, and your ability to reach the notes and range can't be what it was if you don't spend time cultivating your talent.

Recalling it all now makes me incredibly nostalgic for how steeped in music my life was at one time. It also makes me a little sad. Sometimes I think I made a choice to leave behind a part of myself. I often think about what might have been had I pursued my passion. *Would I have become a professional singer? Would I have performed in musical theater? Would I have become a clarinetist with the Toronto Symphony Orchestra?* My husband and I were members of the TSO in the early years of our marriage, and I would often find myself listening to and watching the orchestra and daydreaming about what it would be like to be on that stage.

Music was a fundamental part of my upbringing and education. I believe that it played a significant role in my academic success and love for school. It gave me tremendous confidence and taught me both discipline and how to live in the flow of my creativity. The former is important; the latter is priceless. Now that I am a mother, I see what a gift music is to a child, how it opens up and sparks their creativity, curiosity, wonder, and self-love. I want my son's childhood and youth to be filled with music, partly because it was my experience but mostly because of the passion and talent for music *he* is already demonstrating. And the beauty of it is that if, in the future, he is at a crossroads and considering pursuing a career in music over a more traditional path, I will help him to understand that one is not better than the other and that choosing the latter does not have to mean giving up the former. I saw a life in music and a career as a lawyer as mutually exclusive. It did not have to be that way.

Pause, reflect, lean in

- *Were you asked "What do you want to be when you grow up" as a child? If so, how did you answer that question?*

- *Is there a relationship between what your answer was and what your career/careers has/have been as an adult?*

- *What is something—for example, dancing, singing, playing a sport—you wish you had continued into adulthood? Do you think it would still be a part of your life today?*

- *What would it feel like to carve out even fifteen minutes a day to cultivate your passion?*

Chapter Six

Expectations and Impostor Syndrome

I was the first person in my family to attend university. Being accepted to the University of Toronto, one of the most prestigious institutions of higher learning in North America and perhaps the world, made me incredibly happy and proud. However, it also made me feel unworthy, particularly as I commenced the first year of my undergraduate degree.

Did I really deserve to be there? Surely my peers were from families whose parents were university graduates. What business did a first-generation Canadian born to parents who immigrated from a small village on the other side of the world have attending university and the *University of Toronto*, no less?

What did I do? I buried the feelings of unworthiness. In the large lecture halls of thousands of students, in the endless reading, in the busy weeks of studying, in working part time, in socializing with my friends during the little time that I had to do so, and in spending time with my family. I was still living at home and commuting the hour each way to and from the downtown Toronto campus. I loved my classes, enjoyed what I was learning, and excelled. I had terrific professors, met interesting people, and made wonderful friendships.

But underneath it all, I felt twinges of unworthiness. I felt uncomfortable telling people that I was a student at the St. George Campus of the University of Toronto. Can you imagine? I worked extremely hard to get to where I was. I was a first-generation Canadian and the first one in my family to attend university, and I felt "unworthy." I felt as if I should not talk about what I was doing "too much" because people would think poorly of me, and so I didn't. I believed that if I wore this part of my life with pride, I'd be looked down upon.

Reflecting on my university years, I see how I changed from a student who loved engaging in the classroom and using her voice. In high school (and before then), I was that student. However, in university, and particularly in the first year when classes were very large and were more of a lecture format, student participation was less frequent. I became quieter, more subdued. I spent a lot of time alone on campus between classes. I would run into a friend or two regularly; however, large parts of my day were spent alone, which was the case for my first two years of my three-year degree. In my third year, I had a mix of large lecture hall classes and smaller groups where in the cases of the latter, discussion and student participation was more of the norm. By the end of my degree, I didn't speak up in class as often as I once did, and when I did, I felt nervous. I was also less likely to seek out opportunities to engage with other students and to pursue extracurricular activities. I turned inward.

Overall, I did very well during my undergraduate program. But I can recall a few experiences that were less than stellar, yet unexpectedly gratifying. I took a first-year English literature course because I really enjoyed my English classes in high school and loved literature. I had an eccentric and rather abrupt professor (I will call him Professor C) who had a striking physical resemblance to the actor John Cleese. Alas, he did not seem to share his personality or humor. I remember receiving my first paper back from the professor with a big C+ written at the top and a tidy little typed note that referred to my writing as "Chatty Cathy language." The horror. That was step one. Step two entailed each student meeting with Professor C individually during his office hours *to discuss their paper*. Oh, how I dreaded that meeting! In the end, the meeting was not so bad as Professor C confessed that perhaps he had challenged us too much with our first assignment. Did I mention that we had to read a book that was written entirely in old English and then write a paper about it? To this day, I cannot recall the title of the book or what it was about. Come to think of it, I don't believe I ever fully understood what it was about. Overall, I enjoyed the course very much, as it introduced me to several beloved writers including Alice Munro and George Eliot. I remember when, on Professor C's recommendations to our class, I excitedly searched magazine shops (yes, those existed in 1992) for a copy of *The New Yorker* magazine that published an excerpt from Alice Munro's collection *Open Secrets*, finally finding it at a shop in Yorkville, a shopping district in Toronto. Before that day, I had never heard of Alice Munro or *The New Yorker*. I now have all of Alice Munro's short story collections, and I have subscribed to *The New Yorker* a few times. It was a university class I would never forget.

When I learned that I had been accepted to the Faculty of Law at the University of Toronto, I was proud, excited, and nervous as hell. Wrapped up with the feelings that I had worked hard and deserved to attend this law school were feelings of unworthiness and that only affluent students whose parents were university graduates (with more than one degree) were entitled to be there.

Have you seen the film *The Paper Chase*? It was released in 1973, the year of my birth. The film is about an intelligent and eager first-year student at Harvard Law School and his perception of and desire to obtain the approval of his contracts professor who has taught at the school for forty years and who inspires awe and fear in his students. I expected that the film would generate excitement within me about starting law school, but it ended up having the opposite effect. After years of being in classes of hundreds, I dreaded being exposed to the Socratic method in smaller classes.

I had taken a year off between my undergraduate degree and law degree. I needed the break, but the decision was also financially motivated. Law school was more expensive than my undergraduate education had been, although it was a small fraction of the cost it is today. I wanted to live on campus because I felt I had missed out on this experience during my undergraduate years. Although I had held a part-time job from the age of fifteen and throughout university, I still felt that I relied on my parents a lot and did not really know how to take care of myself. I also didn't have much privacy at home, as I shared a room with my younger sister my whole life. I wanted to meet new people, expand my experiences, gain independence, and just grow. My parents were supportive but made it known that I would need to contribute to the cost of residence if living there was something I wanted to do. And when I set my mind to something, I made it happen.

My "gap year" turned out to be a welcome respite from academics. I enjoyed my break from school and loved working. I met new people and cultivated new friendships. I was eventually promoted to assistant manager of the retail store where I was responsible for hiring staff in addition to my other responsibilities. I enjoyed this time, but I also missed being a student and was excited about planning my first year of law school.

When it came time to consider where I would be living for law school, a nontraditional residence appealed to me. I chose a graduate residence that was part of Victoria College at the University of Toronto and was located across the street from the law school. The graduate residence would enable me to meet others at various stages of their second degree, including people outside of law school. I met people from the law school, including second- and third-years, and students at the Faculty of Music and the Faculty of Education (OISE), to name a few. It was great. I was living an adventure that I did not get to experience during my undergraduate years. My two years living on campus were amazing. I decided to move back home and commute for my third year of law school.

The socioeconomic background of many of my peers in my first year of law school was unlike my own. Many of my peers received a private school education and grew up spending summers away at camp. Unlike my undergraduate experience, the law school was very small. I was no longer one in a sea of hundreds in a class, or one of thousands in a year. There were approximately 120 students in my entire first-year class. I recognized and knew nearly all of them by name. It was nice in some ways, but it also made me more visible and my impostor syndrome more pronounced.

Things improved in my second and third years as I got to know my peers and became close friends with many of them. I not only grew into my mid-twenties by that time, but I also grew into my self-worth, ability, and identity as a law student with hopes, dreams, and goals for the future.

My trajectory to law school was, in some ways, unexpected. My parents immigrated to Canada in their early twenties with a limited formal education and lacking in the opportunities that they would later zealously safeguard for their three children. Yet, in other ways, it was entirely predictable. I was always an achiever—a high-achiever, very disciplined, and a lover of learning. I achieved terrific marks in university, had a stellar grade point average, took the subjects that I enjoyed, and did exceptionally well. I suppose I also had the traits of what one "expects" of a lawyer. I was logical, articulate, driven, assertive, a persuasive writer and speaker, a clear thinker, and a problem solver.

But I was also creative, musical, a lover of the arts and literature, and a dreamer. I tended to see people and the world through rose-colored glasses. I could be incredibly sensitive and often took things personally. I had a positive outlook when it came to others around me and in the ability of the human spirit to love and serve. But when it came to myself, I had no hesitation in being judgmental and critical.

Although I may have presented as someone self-assured and confident, I was quite introverted. I often shied away from social situations and preferred a quiet night at home, listening to music, and enjoying a novel. Invitations to parties were anxiety-provoking. The anxiety did not stop me from going (in most cases). I went to my fair share of parties, but I often ended up working myself up into a state before arriving and then spending the first thirty minutes trying to relax and unwind the knots in my stomach and the insecurities in my mind with the help of a glass of wine. I also habitually sought out the approval of others. How people perceived me was important to me, and I worried about disappointing those who thought highly of me and not living up to their expectations (and my own).

When I was accepted to the University of Toronto Faculty of Arts and Science, those who knew me were impressed but also not surprised in the least. When I graduated with the Dean's List standing, this achievement was also expected and applauded. When I applied to and was accepted to my choice of law schools, including my first choice, the Faculty of Law at the University of Toronto, I was admired.

How did I feel about all of it? I was happy and excited but also scared. I was an overachiever my whole life. And I would continue to achieve. How could I let people down by failing now?

Although my parents wanted us to receive a university education, the message they conveyed and instilled in each of us was that our life path is shaped by our own unique desires and dreams. I was incredibly thankful for this message when I developed the maturity to fully understand it. And now that I have a child of my own, I am even more grateful for having parents who truly gave us the space to grow and forge our own life path, nurturing and encouraging us every step of the way.

Having said this, on some level, my desire and drive to become a lawyer *also* became about not disappointing those who expected me to excel and maintaining the approval of those who already had a certain impression of me—my family, my extended family, my friends, my teachers, and my peers. More than anything, going to law school and pursuing a career in law was about holding my word to myself from the moment I declared that I wanted to be a lawyer at age twelve or thirteen. It was my way of connecting the dots to its logical conclusion.

The goal of most first-year law students was to land a summer position on Bay Street in Toronto (i.e., at a large corporate law firm). I half-heartedly applied to a handful of firms and had two or three interviews. I was not hired. Although I cannot say I was disappointed, as I did not feel strongly about working at a law firm over the summer, the fact that I was unable to secure a position did leave me feeling less worthy than my peers. After all, securing a position at a law firm is what first-year law students were supposed to do. And the overachiever in me felt disappointed; the impostor syndrome crept back up again.

I had worked at the Grand & Toy store at the mall close to my childhood home throughout most of high school and during my undergraduate degree. When I took a gap year before beginning law school, I spent approximately four months managing that particular store until it closed down and I was able to secure an assistant managerial position at another location. I ended up quite happily working at a third Grand & Toy store the summer after my first year of law school, spearheading a new project that made for an interesting experience.

After my second year of law school, I spent the summer working for two amazing lawyers who practiced labor and employment law as well as human rights law. I mainly conducted research and prepared memoranda, but I was also able to shadow the two lawyers in meetings and arbitration hearings and do some client intake work. To say that experience was unforgettable would be an understatement. I will also be forever grateful to the two women who hired me, effectively creating a position for me and giving me my first taste of working at a law firm.

When I graduated from the Faculty of Law, I completed my articles at a full-service firm in downtown Toronto. Many of my peers had landed corporate law summer-student positions either for corporate/commercial litigation firms or as in-house counsel. I may not have been paid a salary that rivaled theirs, but I still earned a lot more than I had ever earned before, worked with and was mentored by wonderful people, and was given tons of responsibility. I was able to go to court regularly, shadowing phenomenal lawyers and learning a great deal about the law. I even had the chance to argue motions before a master in civil and commercial court several times and appear in criminal set-date court at Old City Hall. When I successfully argued my first motion, opposing counsel congratulated me and told me he had been practicing for five years and that he learned a thing or two from me that day. I was stunned.

Pause, reflect, lean in

- *Can you recall a moment in your life where you may have felt like an impostor? Why?*
- *What are some traits and qualities that you might have repressed for fear of what people may say?*
- *Who would you be if you released the expectations and agendas placed on you by others?*
- *Can you recall moments in your life where you allowed yourself to be who you are and showed up unapologetically? How did that feel?*

Chapter Seven

I Did It! I Became a Lawyer

I was excited to begin my career in family law, but I was also incredibly nervous. I started the position about a month before my call to the Bar of Ontario, an event that I will always remember. As a new associate, I had a decent salary, a comfortable office, a parking pass for when I bought my first car (and paid for outright) eight months into my first year of practice, and eventually, my own assistant. I was able to afford nice clothes and accessories, take regular vacations and stay in upscale accommodations, dine out frequently, and have memberships to the symphony and theater. My husband and I were able to purchase our first home three years after I began my career. We extensively renovated it piece by piece and paid down its mortgage within six years.

All of these achievements felt good; I believed I had earned them. What I had accomplished was the byproduct of planning, discipline, and determination. I was proud of my success, but I didn't really like to talk about it. I still had trouble owning my accomplishments; in fact, I found it much easier to downplay them. I never forgot, for a moment, where I came from and the many sacrifices my parents had made to give us a life where we were well cared for and provided for—physically and emotionally. We were exceptionally and unconditionally loved and always encouraged to pursue our dreams and become whoever we wanted.

Being acknowledged, liked, and respected is a basic human need. It feels good to be liked. I want people to think highly of me. I want people to be pleased with my accomplishments. Who doesn't want the same for themselves? It doesn't make us selfish, but it does make us human. It is natural to desire the approval of others, to wish for the acceptance of our family and peers. But it can also hinder our growth. Fearing the disappointment of others or worrying about falling short of expectations, no matter how well intended those expectations and the desire to meet them are, can stifle your own progress and evolution. Seeking external validation and approval before seeking inner validation on our path of growth can keep us constrained, forever playing small. Not living up to our greatest potential. Not following our wildest dreams and desires. It can keep us from living with intention. And living without intention is a compromised life, indeed.

Despite the hurdles that came along with being a new lawyer, I was excited and happy to continue pursuing my career. On the one hand,

I was doing work that motivated and challenged me, work that was interesting and made me feel like I was providing value to my clients who were experiencing one of the most difficult and painful events of their lives. On the other hand, it was not easy to reconcile these feelings with the stressors and pressures that come with being a lawyer. For example, dealing with the difficult and sometimes unrealistic expectations of clients, managing the diverse personalities of opposing counsel, judges, and clients, as well as being available to your client while trying to maintain your own boundaries outside of the office (a lawyer's email inbox is quite the place—it's a party that never ends). I remember the struggle of answering emails in a timely and professional manner that still protected my privacy and boundaries and avoided sending a message to my clients that I was available around the clock and on weekends. I remember the challenge of communicating firmly with opposing counsel while remaining professional and not taking positions and statements personally.

A challenge that I understand is common among lawyers, particularly ones who are new to the profession, is that of aligning with the client personally or taking up their cause. A family lawyer should be their client's advocate, legal advisor, and representative, but they should also be a voice of reason, not their client's mouthpiece or cheerleader. However, it does entail doing so compassionately and humanely. I learned that it was possible to be kind, compassionate, and understanding of my client's experience while remaining professional and within the scope of a lawyer's responsibilities and maintaining integrity with my boundaries. I also observed that practicing family law without compassion and humanity does a serious disservice to your client and doesn't make your job particularly likable, nor does it make you feel good about getting up in the morning and beginning your day.

Learning from the wonderful mentors that I have had during my legal career is something I will never forget and for which I am grateful. However, evolving into my own self-worth as a professional, as a strong, ethical, effective advocate who practiced with integrity, was extremely important to me. I also recall the challenges of leaving my work at the office and not bringing it home with me. I am not referring to the occasions when I physically took file work home with me on weekends, for example (a regular event, particularly in my formative years). I am referring to the psychological piece—allowing the weight of my legal responsibilities to regularly permeate into my personal life, my family life. It is far more challenging than it sounds, perhaps because it happens subtly at first without you even being aware of it. And before you realize it, your personal life revolves around your work, and it becomes a vicious cycle to break out of unless you consciously and conscientiously choose to keep the two separate.

I enjoyed practicing law. I loved working with my clients to determine their rights and obligations and to help them close an often incredibly painful chapter of their life so that they could move forward on their journey. I loved oral and written advocacy, interpreting and applying the law, and having a hand in shaping the law. I loved witnessing how my advocacy translated into negotiated resolutions and desired court outcomes. I felt proud of myself for pursuing a career that flowed from my years of education and for achieving my dream. However, as time went on, I became curious about what else I could do with my life. I was feeling the nudges and hearing the regular whispers: "Write a book, a novel, a memoir," "Get your master's degree and teach," "Retrain and explore something different," "Go out on your own and launch a firm." I would fantasize about taking steps in one or more of these directions and imagine what my life could become.

Instead of allowing the whispers to crescendo, I would hush them with a quiet but firm "Now isn't the best time" or "Now is the time to *really* work, to solidify my reputation as a lawyer, to make money. I'd love to do those things *later, when I have kids, when my son is older, in the future, but not now.*" The problem with this way of thinking is that "later" inevitably becomes "never." And we all know that someday isn't a day. You're working hard, making a great living, accumulating savings, improving your home, keeping busy, trying to get pregnant, pursuing assisted reproduction, pursuing adoption, feeling tired, losing the passion, going through the motions and simply existing.

Before you know it, those vibrant dreams are muted and buried by all the busyness and noise we like to think of as "life." And without you even realizing it, "one day" has come and gone. And that is an existence I wouldn't wish upon anyone. Life is meant to be lived, wholeheartedly, with intention, excitement, joy, and fulfillment. And denying your soul nudges, dampening your light, quieting the crescendo that wants to be heard and seen is not any way to live, to be who you are.

Pause, reflect, lean in

- *When was the last time you felt or heard any nudges and whispers?*

- *What have they told you?*

- *How did you respond? Did you act on them?*

- *If you did act on them, what happened? If you didn't, what do you think was the reason?*

- *What would you have done differently, if at all?*

Chapter Eight

First Comes Love, Then Comes Marriage, Then Comes . . .

I will be celebrating my nineteenth wedding anniversary a month after the launch of this book. Nineteen years of marriage. Twenty-three years as a couple. In a blink of an eye.

I have been sleeping beside the same person for two decades.

Whoa.

How exactly did that happen?

It was 1996. *Seinfeld*, *Friends*, and *ER* were the most popular shows on television, and I was a first-year student at the University of Toronto Faculty of Law.

As I stated earlier, I had moved out of my childhood home and into a graduate residence on the university campus in downtown Toronto across the street from the law school. In some ways, I was experiencing the emotions of someone about four years younger, who was moving into a university residence for the first time—except I was doing it at age twenty-three and when I was starting my second degree. I was excited, nervous, and scared, all at the same time.

My small graduate residence was in an architecturally stunning building of four floors and fourteen rooms in the Victoria College campus of the university. The building was constructed in 1931 and renovations completed in 1995, the year before I moved in. If you are familiar with this part of the St. George Campus, you will probably be familiar with what I am describing. I had my own room on the first floor and shared a full bathroom with my "suite mate," the woman in the room next door. I became close friends with a woman who lived on the fourth floor and was studying at the Faculty of Music. One Friday evening, as I was on my way to our house movie night, I almost collided with a dark-haired guy who had just walked into the building. He was tall, definitely a few inches taller than I am (and I'm five foot ten), and he was wearing a black leather biker jacket and Doc Martens. Did I mention that I was wearing pajama shorts? Yep. He smiled and said hi, and I think I said hi back although I was likely too flustered to even articulate this greeting. I didn't know who this guy was, but I did know that he didn't live in the building. A moment later, my friend was introducing me to her older brother, Jeff, who, as it turns out, I would begin dating the following year and marry a few years later.

I probably would never have met Jeff had I not known his sister. We were studying in different fields. Jeff was pursuing his master's degree in molecular genetics, and I was in law school. Our paths crossed a few more times later that year and more often during the following year. Jeff eventually asked me out to lunch. I recall we had pizza at an intimate restaurant on Baldwin Street. Love soon blossomed, and by the time I was taking the final section of the Bar Admission Course, we were living together. Our parents disapproved of our new living arrangement, and for this reason, we did not tell many people. Getting engaged shortly after we moved in together made our decision easier for our parents to accept and allayed our feelings that we had disappointed them.

I applied to a handful of firms, all small boutique firms specializing in one or two areas. I focused on human rights, employment law, and family law firms. I secured interviews at two reputable family law firms in Toronto, and one made me an offer. I spent the next nineteen years working at that firm. It was where I first had the incredible opportunity to be mentored by one of the country's leading family lawyers, to work with wonderful lawyers, some of whom became close friends, and where I established myself.

Jeff and I got married when I was twenty-nine and he was thirty, about a year and a half after I was called to the Bar. My husband and I made what we then believed was the prudent decision to postpone starting a family for a few years. We were very happy. Our marriage was strong. We both had demanding careers. Jeff was completing a lengthy and demanding PhD in neuroscience and physiology, and I was working eleven- or twelve-hour days at a busy firm. We made it work. We went out to dinner every Friday. We went to jazz clubs regularly. We socialized with friends. We enjoyed frequent vacations. We planned our vacations meticulously and strategically, as otherwise my career, in particular, would not have left much time at all for an escape. Our focus was on ourselves and our careers. Life was pretty good, but it was not a "good time" to introduce children into the mix.

At the time, our marriage was about making responsible financial decisions, spending our time the way that we wanted, and pursuing our careers and interests. We envisioned a life with children—one day. We were not in a hurry to become parents. We believed that life had to unfold a certain way before introducing children into our family: we had to be established in our jobs, have a certain level of savings, own our first home, and be well on our way to paying off our mortgage. Quite the to-do list, isn't it?

We enjoyed our life together. We accomplished those important financial goals and had stability. But our reasons for delaying the family piece were rooted in a lot more than meeting goals and having stability. Jeff and I were both raised in families where our mothers stayed home. Jeff's mom did have a career for several years but one where she had a certain level of flexibility. My mom was a stay-at-home mother throughout my childhood except for when she briefly held a part-time job after my father lost his job when I was ten years of age. Although I had two degrees and thought of myself as a "career woman" and "independent," I identified with my mother's role in our family. I looked up to her and admired her greatly. My programming, something that I likely was not even conscious of having, told me that being a mother meant devoting yourself to your children in a way that required you to be physically present for them at home—perhaps not all day, but certainly in the mornings in preparing them for school and welcoming them and caring for them when they returned home from their day. There was a part of me that could not reconcile that programming and belief system with the reality of what my career looked like at that time. Perhaps that also played into why it was "not the right time" to start a family.

You can probably guess what happened next.

When we decided that the time was "right," it . . . wasn't.

I wasn't getting pregnant. Despite having regular periods since my first menses at age fourteen and a predictable cycle, that monthly visitor became a permanent monthly return guest, and so did my crushing disappointment. I'd ask myself, "Why me?" or "Why not me?" quite a bit over the coming years. Those words became embedded in my vocabulary. They were like breathing. Isn't it strange that the things we most long for seem to be perpetually out of reach, yet the things we don't seek seem to fall into our lives with ease?

Trying to have a baby is *trying.*

The word "trying" has an interesting meaning. Trying as in

attempting. *Trying* as in difficult, challenging. The connotation of the word's second usage signifies strife, conflict, struggle. I never really thought of this connotation before. The phrase that is used by just about everyone who is working toward conception is synonymous with strife. The language we use—toward ourselves and others—is powerful and shapes our consciousness. Can you imagine the difference it could make to replace this language with something lighter and easier?

Trying to get pregnant inevitably changes your relationship with your spouse. Your moments together become planned around a purpose. You are so focused on the goal of conceiving a child that you ignore everything else that is happening around you, including what is no longer happening between the two of you (intimacy, connection, and spontaneous joy). You are so attached to the outcome of having a baby, you long for it to such a degree, that you don't even realize that the very foundation you have spent years building and cultivating with each other is slowly and systematically being chipped and eroded from under you.

Sounds dramatic, doesn't it? Maybe a little. But if you have traveled the infertility journey then it may just resonate with you.

Don't get me wrong: Jeff and I loved each other and had a solid marriage, but our relationship really changed when we were *trying* but not *getting* pregnant. There was this sharpness to it, the edges lost their softness, and being in a marriage felt hard. I missed our flow, our spontaneity, our emotional connection. It's not possible for our relationship to have remained the same when we, as individuals, had evolved in the process.

A healthy marriage is built on connectedness, a cadence, and being able to find and create joy *despite* and *through* the challenges of daily life. The substance of a relationship, the heart of what makes it work, is what ties and holds it together, particularly during moments of difficulty. However, the theme of our marriage, our relationship, became centered on loss . . . and soon *lack* became a constant focus. Our interactions were fueled by what was *missing* and what we were so desperately *trying* to create. And although we felt incredibly alone, the irony was that we were not alone because of the ever-present elephant in the room—the void of sorrow that we were unable to fill.

An underlying tension permeated our interactions. It is as if we were permanently walking on eggshells, careful not to set off a cascade of emotions that we would be unable to control. It is easy to take for granted the relaxed, spontaneous feeling and ease of a marriage. A couple falls into a rhythm and that rhythm is all consuming. It may be grounded in familiar, predictable routines, but it is sustained and rejuvenated by spontaneity, fun, surprise, and unplanned moments. When you are on a mission to conceive, the cadence of ease and flow, the balance of familiar and spontaneous, becomes fundamentally disrupted. And the saddest part is that you do not realize it is happening until it has already happened, and often, when it is too late to do anything about it.

Timing intimacy around your ovulation cycle is not exciting. It is tedious and frustrating. And doing it for any length of time is excruciatingly draining. I am going to be very frank. I began to dread having sex with my husband. And when we were having sex, the passion wasn't there. Underlying the act of making love was the fear of failure. Fear of being inadequate, not enough. Instead of feeling emotionally and physically connected to my partner, I was consumed with anxiety. There were even times that I would break down in tears while we were being intimate. I also started experiencing pain during intercourse, which I did not understand at the time was a physiological response to the tremendous stress and worry I felt about conception. It all made me feel disconnected from my husband and extremely inadequate as a woman.

Marriage was once thought of as the vehicle to procreation. The purpose of marriage was to populate the human race. Who am I kidding? Many still view it that way. While this way of thinking is considered "outdated" by many in modern society, it is astounding how many people believe that the goal of a newly married couple is to conceive on their wedding night (or within the first few months of marriage anyway). I remember, all too well, comments like, "You've been married for, what, six months now? When are you going to have a baby?" It was almost a given that newly married couples would be asked this type of question. Once again, societal expectations and norms dictate the quality of life we live as humans, the milestones that are deemed as worthy, and the timelines on which we experience those milestones.

As time went on and with each anniversary we celebrated, these questions and comments began to affect me in a different way. I felt that something was wrong—with me. I felt incomplete and damaged. I felt that I was a less worthy wife and individual.

My self-image as a woman and a wife were not the only things affected. For a time, I began to question my competence and worth as a lawyer. Yes, the very thing that I had set my mind to accomplishing, my big goal (effectively since childhood), that thing that I was able to achieve and that I believed in my heart of hearts to be good at, was under attack—by my own internal narrative. It may not sound particularly rational, but when you really think about it, what are limiting beliefs? I had crafted a theory and concluded that *I was less of a family lawyer because I was not a parent.*

Wait. What?

I can think of several family lawyers I have met over the years who are not parents—both men and women. Did I think of them as any less of a lawyer because of their parenting status? Of course not. And yet, I held myself to an irrational standard. I had created a compelling internal narrative that my childlessness was affecting my ability to practice law, that I could not possibly understand my clients (those clients who had children) and their challenges (i.e., parenting issues) and advocate for them well *because I did not share one of their characteristics: parenthood.*

When those clients struggled with parenting and had difficulty adjusting to their children spending time between two homes, who was I to provide them with advice when I was not a parent myself? Who was I to say anything when I was assessing the situation through the eyes of someone—family lawyer or not—who was childless? How could I possibly understand a father's pleas to spend more time with his young children when I did not have a child of my own? How could I understand a mother's concerns that her spouse was disrespecting the residential schedule and maligning her to and in front of their children as a way to control and pressure her to accede to his position in court? How could I possibly empathize, understand, and advocate properly when I was not a parent?

Now, some would say that looking at the situation through only the lens of a lawyer made it *easier* to do my job without allowing personal biases or experiences to get in the way of my advocacy. However, at the time, I did not view it this way. At the time, I felt inadequate, "less of" a woman, wife, *and* lawyer.

I know now that my worth as a human being, as a woman, is not tied to my ability to have children. Your accomplishments—your very core essence—do not depend on whether or not you have children. Experiencing any sort of personal challenge can often feel overwhelming and debilitating. Here is where the power of standing in your worth and personal power is truly magical and life changing. Know that your worth is inherent. It just is. It isn't and never will be connected to your circumstances. That you can still be an incredibly nurturing human being and not be a parent or even desire parenthood. That you can be extremely empathetic to another's situation and challenges without being a parent. So, promise yourself that no matter what, you will lean into your personal power, love yourself and your body, stand in your worth, and not let anyone or anything else dictate the timelines of your life. Because if there is one thing I've learned, it is this: Everything unfolds wildly, in its own precious time, and when you receive your heart's desire, you'll know that the journey it took to get there was worthwhile.

Pause, reflect, lean in

- *Can you recall a time in your life where you felt or were made to feel "less than," "not enough?"*
- *How did you navigate that time? What did you feel?*
- *What are some societal expectations that weigh heavily on your mind? Why?*
- *If societal ideals weren't a thing, what would you do? Who would you be? How would you treat yourself?*
- *Take a moment and write down all the incredible things you've accomplished—personally and professionally. And now, repeat after me: I AM . . . (capable, worthy, enough, loving, kind, other affirmative language).*

Chapter Nine

The Anguish of Infertility

When we were trying to have a baby, it seemed that everyone around us was pregnant. Suddenly there were expectant mothers *everywhere*.

Everywhere I looked, I was reminded of what I did not have: there were pregnant women walking down the street, pregnant women at the grocery store, women taking pregnancy tests in television commercials (have you noticed how common these are?), pregnant lawyers at court, pregnant colleagues at the office, pregnant cousins, pregnant friends, baby shower invitations, baby showers at the office, baby gender-reveal celebrations, christening invitations, first birthday invitations, women pushing strollers down the street, colleagues at the office with their infants in tow. While I feigned happiness and offered the obligatory smiles, hugs, and congratulatory wishes, I was crumbling inside, fighting back tears, and silently screaming. If you are currently navigating a similar season in your life, my heart is with you. I see you.

Shopping for baby shower gifts can be suffocating for someone whose fertility journey is not unfolding the way that they wish. I used to do it. I'd go to the store, print off the list from one of the kiosks or print it at home and take it with me, then go about choosing a gift for the expectant mother and her unborn child. I could have ordered the item, or enclosed money or a gift card, but I believed I was supposed to choose the gift myself for it to be meaningful, particularly for a close friend or relative.

Spending thirty minutes in a Babies "R" Us surrounded by onesies, pajamas, blankets, strollers, carriers, baby bottles, breast pumps, and toys is overwhelming for a woman who is experiencing infertility. It was inevitable that I left the store feeling far worse than when I had arrived, my despair highlighted for me once more.

Speaking to others about your fertility journey can be very uncomfortable, even painful. To be clear, for the most part, I was surrounded by family and friends who were extremely supportive and sensitive to what I was going through. However, outside of these, there were also experiences and conversations that left me feeling nothing like someone who was being supported or understood or loved. Those conversations mirrored or were a variation of the following:

"So, how many children do you have?"

"Actually, I don't have children."

"Oh. Don't you want children?"

"Yes, we do. What I meant is that we don't have children yet."

"What are you waiting for? Life goes by really quickly."

"That's true, but we are both really busy right now with work, so it's not the best time to start a family."

"Well, don't wait too long!"

Other times, the conversation went something like this:

"No kids?"

"Not yet."

"Really? Why not?"

"My career keeps me really busy, so it's not the best time."

"Well, you'll have to decide what's more important, you know?"

Or like this:

"Sure, we want to have kids, but we are both at the start of our careers, so we're waiting for now."

"Well, you don't want to wait too long. It will probably get harder to have a baby the longer you wait."

And sometimes like this:

"Don't you want to be a mom?"

"I do, but we haven't been able to get pregnant yet."

"Oh, are you okay? Have you spoken to your doctor about it?"

(hmm)

Or:

"You know, there are specialists you can see . . . "

(yep)

Or:

"Have you thought about adopting? There are so many children who need a home."

(ugh)

It is *really, really hard* to listen to these questions and statements. It's even harder when the person you are speaking with is someone you know. When someone you have just met asks these types of questions, it is easier to not pay them much heed. But when it is someone you care about, someone you respect, someone with whom you have any history, the comments hit hard and cut deep. Simply put, it is nobody's business as to whether you're planning on having kids, or desire kids, or want to continue expanding your family.

It is equally difficult to listen to someone profess to be knowledgeable about conception and fertility simply because they have given birth. And it is *torturous* to listen to someone attempt to draw conclusions about your life and values and priorities that they have no damn right or basis to draw.

In the beginning, the questions and comments made me uncomfortable. I would lower my gaze, feeling judged, embarrassed by, and ashamed about the answers I was giving.

Then the questions and comments made me incredibly sad. I lived every day with the pain of not being able to have a child. These conversations only highlighted the gaping hole in my life. I don't know how many times I had to fight back tears and pretend that it was somehow acceptable for this person to be asking such personal questions and drawing such insensitive and sometimes insulting conclusions.

Until finally, the comments and questions began to infuriate me. They angered me to the point that I wanted to punch the person. I am embarrassed to admit it, but it's true. In one such instance when I was asked, "Don't you want children?" I retorted with, "Sure I do, but it's not quite the same thing as deciding to get a puppy or a kitten, don't you think?" while staring the person directly in the eye and without missing a beat.

Can you really blame me?

Here's the thing:
All it would have taken is for the person who had the audacity to ask the said question to briefly put themselves in the shoes of the woman, me, standing opposite them, and to gather up a modicum of sensitivity *to support* rather than comment and *to empathize* rather than instruct, judge, and pontificate.

It will happen when you stop trying.

I was married for thirteen years before I became a mother. I probably heard "It will happen when you stop trying" dozens, maybe hundreds (perhaps it felt like hundreds) of times in those thirteen years. Even though it did ultimately happen for us when we were no longer trying, I understand, all too well, how unhelpful those words are. No one, and I mean no one, should profess to know if or when someone will have a child. Passing comments like "It will happen when you stop trying" give the person on the receiving end of your comment absolutely no reassurance that "it will happen" *ever*. It also minimizes their infertility experience, relegating it to something simple and insignificant. As you read this book, you will see that I say a lot about the relationship between one's mindset and their fertility journey. While it is important to understand this relationship, I am not suggesting that infertility is as straightforward as changing the way you think about your journey. Infertility is extraordinarily complex, hence the term "unexplained infertility." And if a medical doctor, a gynecologist, an obstetrician, *or a fertility expert* cannot explain why someone is not getting pregnant, why would you even attempt to do so?

Imagine what it feels like to live your life anticipating and avoiding the pain, shame, and embarrassment that could flow from an innocent conversation or exchange? I began dreading functions and events where I would run into relatives and family friends that I saw infrequently. What I really dreaded were the questions and commentary that would inevitably come blasting at me. "Are you the sister *with* children or *without*?" was a popular one as was "Are you the one with two kids?" I am not exaggerating when I say that I can clearly recall instances where I was asked *each of these questions* by the same person over a period of a few years. I'm dead serious. The words cut deep as did my responses: "Actually, I'm the sister without children" or "No, I'm the other one, the one without kids." I didn't have to answer this way. I could have answered very differently, but I did not have the luxury of my present awareness. The "I really don't give a shit what you think about my answer" attitude at the time I was navigating one of the most difficult journeys of my life hadn't yet been born.

I once became physically ill with severe nausea and a pounding headache rivaling migraine intensity because of the level of anxiety I experienced *before* attending a baby shower. What ultimately got me there was quite literally forcing myself to think of the innocent unborn baby who meant no harm and that a part of me truly did want to celebrate and rejoice in the expectation of welcoming them into this world. I'm proud of myself for changing the narrative that way, for flipping the script, if you will. But it was not easy to do, and I really did not need to do it to myself. *I deserved more.* I deserved to give myself grace, to allow myself the space to sit that one out, even if it meant disappointing a few people. *I deserved better.* And now, I know that.

I understand that people mean well and that it is difficult to understand, let alone to articulate support and compassion when interacting with someone who is experiencing infertility. Unless you have experienced it yourself, how could you truly understand the pain and anguish and complex feelings that one goes through? I get it. I do. But there are things you *can* do and there are ways you can show up for the person you care about with kindness and empathy. A good rule is to err on the side of less is more, meaning that it is better to say less than try and fill up the conversation with probing questions. Listening actively and simply holding space for the friend/colleague/sister/cousin/peer goes an incredibly long way.

The next time you find yourself interacting with someone experiencing fertility challenges or perhaps if you are experiencing them yourself, I want you to read these words out loud to yourself. There is power in upholding emotional, physical, and energetic boundaries, especially if you or someone you know is navigating these challenges.

> When you are seeing me as less than ecstatic about the news of your pregnancy or the birth of your child, it does not mean that I am not happy for you. It means that I am sad *for myself.*
>
> My decision to sit out the event is not about you. It is not about wanting to make your day any less enjoyable, it is not about sending anyone a message, it is not about desiring someone's pity. It is about self-preservation and self-love.

Years ago, I was not able to articulate these sentiments to even myself, but I see it so clearly now. I was not unhappy about my friend or colleague's pregnancy news. I was feeling sad for myself. I did not deserve to feel guilty. I deserved self-compassion and self-love.

> When my presence at your baby shower or your child's first birthday party appears subdued, do not take it personally. It is simply a reflection of how I am feeling and the complicated and often conflicting emotions I am navigating within myself as I try to celebrate your joy.

It is not about you. It is about me.

It is about my feelings, my pain, my experience. It has nothing to do with your baby's birth or your child's milestone.

It is something that really has nothing to do with you at all.

It is about my journey, my path, my experience, *and it is my right to feel.*

It is, however, *your duty* as a human being to allow me the space to feel whatever I feel and to give me your blessing to sit this one out.

Don't judge. Don't criticize. Don't resent. Don't hate.

Give me grace. Allow me the space and time. Be kind. Show understanding. Show compassion. Show love.

Pause, reflect, lean in

- *Write a love letter to yourself and your body. Allow it to be free flowing. Pour out your emotions onto paper. Write about all the ways in which your mind/body/soul have supported you and all the things they help you accomplish.*

- *Now write another letter to yourself. This time, list all the unkind things that have been said to you (albeit unintentionally) by others, or even your own negative self-talk. Fold that piece of paper, and with a hand on your heart and with eyes closed, repeat this mantra: "I release this energy, these words, these emotions. I release what doesn't belong to me." Then either burn this paper (keeping safety in mind, of course) or rip it into shreds and dispose of it. You've just had an energetic release.*

Chapter Ten

Assisted Reproduction and Adoption

Both my maternal and paternal grandparents had large families. My mother had four siblings as did my father. Since both my parents came from large families, I always thought that I came from a fertile lineage. Sounds silly now, but that is how I once felt. My point is that I never imagined I would have difficulty conceiving. I don't think anyone expects it. We always hope for smooth sailing in all things life, love, health, and careers.

From the moment of my first period, I have had a regular menstrual cycle, and by regular, I mean precise and predictable. What wasn't normal or typical was the heaviness of my flow and the intense pain I experienced each month. I remember missing school or calling in sick at my part-time job as a teenager because I was in bed, curled up in the fetal position in agony. I remember feeling cramps so intense that I would vomit. I remember taking the subway with a friend in grade eleven after visiting the Toronto Reference Library to complete a school project, when I felt such intense pain that I turned white as a sheet, lost my vision temporarily, and nearly collapsed while on the subway platform. My friend, who was a lot shorter than I, was terrified. Thankfully, I was okay, and she was able to get me home without further incident. While my friends were participating in the same activities they always enjoyed throughout the month, I was sitting these out for at least a couple of days each month, unable to even imagine that kind of normalcy. I was prescribed birth control pills at approximately age eighteen because my periods were interfering with the quality of my life. The pills helped me manage my symptoms.

I was twenty-nine years of age when Jeff and I married. At that time, I was very focused on my career. It wasn't that I really made a conscious decision to choose my career over having children, it simply evolved that way. I was so busy with work, so involved with the demanding and often overwhelming responsibilities of being a lawyer that, for a time anyway, becoming a mother was not on my radar. It was something outside of where I was; it was in the next room, one I would open the door to "soon," when "the time felt right." When we finally believed that the time "was right" to have a baby, it was not happening. We tried to conceive for approximately two years before we saw a fertility specialist. When you are trying to have a baby, two years is an eternity.

And so began the stage of my life that I like to refer to as my stint as a guinea pig—being poked and prodded to find out "what was wrong with me." Tests and laparoscopic surgery (two laparoscopies of my uterus within two years) uncovered that I had mild to moderate endometriosis,[1] a condition that is not discussed enough and that I had until then assumed meant "heavy periods," which I had experienced for many years, well actually, since my menses started.

Although my case wasn't extreme, my diagnosis remained concerning because even milder conditions of endometriosis can affect fertility. The endometriosis, coupled with my age of thirty-seven years at the time, made becoming pregnant "challenging," at best. One of my tests, an uncomfortable procedure called a sonohysterogram, revealed that at the time of testing, my fallopian tube appeared to be blocked. It was possible that my endometriosis was causing scarring that contributed to the blockage, but it was not known with certainty. I learned that scarring and blockages caused by endometriosis can change over time. In my case, it did ultimately change, as the second of two laparoscopies of my uterus a few years later revealed that the fallopian tube was no longer blocked. After the first of such surgeries, my fertility specialist recommended in vitro fertilization (or IVF as commonly referred to), a form of assisted reproduction. I had heard of IVF before, but I had never imagined that I would be sitting in a doctor's office considering it for myself. I had never missed a period,

---

1 Endometriosis is a painful condition that affects up to 10 percent of premenopausal women and 30 to 50 percent of women who struggle with period symptoms, pelvic pain, and infertility. https://pubmed.ncbi.nlm.nih.gov/19196878/

and they were five or six days long. It was like clockwork. But I was having trouble getting pregnant, I had endometriosis, one of my fallopian tubes seemed to be blocked, I was thirty-seven, and the proverbial clock was ticking.

We longed for a child of our own and wanted to become parents more than anything. My doctor explained the IVF procedure and handed us some literature.[2] He left the room to take a phone call, and by the time he returned, we had made the decision to proceed with IVF. The decision was an easy one. And so began more than three years of blood tests, ultrasounds, injections, egg retrievals, embryo transfers, hope, heartache, loss, sadness, resentment, anger, anguish, despair, and exhaustion.

Infertility is a chronic waiting game. Assisted reproduction is also a chronic waiting game. Waiting, month to month, to get pregnant. Waiting for the missed period. Waiting to have sex when you are ovulating. Waiting to get through endless testing. Waiting for the ideal time to begin IVF. Waiting to determine ideal hormone levels. Waiting to determine if your follicles are optimal. Waiting to determine if the eggs retrieved are viable. Waiting to determine if fertilization takes place. Waiting to determine if there is a viable embryo. Waiting to determine the quality of the embryo. Waiting to schedule the optimal

---

2 Did you know that a woman is born with all the eggs she will ever have? In fact, she has those eggs when she is in utero at the embryonic stage. Isn't that fascinating? The female body is truly miraculous. During IVF, mature eggs are collected (retrieved) from ovaries and fertilized by sperm in a laboratory. Then the fertilized egg (embryo) or eggs (embryos) are transferred to the uterus with the goal of having the embryo implant into the uterine wall. The procedure can be done using your own eggs and your partner's sperm. Or IVF may involve eggs, sperm, or embryos from a known or anonymous donor. In some cases, a gestational carrier is used.

time for the embryo transfer procedure. Waiting to determine if there is a pregnancy. Waiting for the first ultrasound appointment. And so on.

We began our assisted reproduction journey with tremendous hope and faith. We wanted to be parents with every element of our beings. We adored and spent a lot of time with our nieces and nephews, and we longed to have children of our own. I was aware that the odds and statistics of getting pregnant through assisted reproduction (at my age, and with endometriosis) were not encouraging, but we were going to travel this path with the belief that at the end of our journey we would have a baby. The alternative wasn't even a thought in our minds and hearts.

The actual IVF process did not frighten or worry me. I did not think twice about the invasive procedures, the injections, blood tests, ultrasounds, egg retrievals, embryo transfers, monitoring, and waiting—so much waiting. I welcomed it with open arms. Not once did I worry about the risks and side effects. All I really thought about was our procedure being successful, visualizing how it would feel to see and feel my belly growing, giving birth, and holding my baby in my arms for the first time.

I remember the look on Jeff's face as he was about to inject me with the hormone medication I was prescribed to suppress ovulation for the first time. He was more nervous than I was. I recall that he apologized to me. In advance. I looked him in the eye and said, "Just do it." He did (I think *he* squeezed his eyes shut at some point) and then let out a huge exhale when he saw me smiling from ear to ear and excitedly dabbing away at the injection site with an alcohol swab.

We got into a nice momentum of steps during that cycle: injections and visits to the clinic for daily blood tests and ultrasounds. I took significant time away from my law practice to complete two of the four IVF cycles we did.

I've heard IVF described as stressful and draining. That was not my experience, at least not with my first cycle. Any nerves and stress over the process were muted by the excitement of doing something that would lead to having a child. Looking back, I was in an ideal mindset before and during that first cycle. I was calm, and my thoughts were fueled by abundance. It was the cumulative effect of the several cycles and their outcomes that was incredibly stressful physically, emotionally, and psychologically.

Our initial IVF attempt was surreal. I remember sitting in the waiting room for my first appointment when I would undergo bloodwork and an internal ultrasound to determine my hormone levels and timing of the start of the cycle. If you've ever had a vaginal ultrasound, then you know that it isn't really a procedure that one looks forward to (much like one doesn't particularly enjoy a gynecological examination or a dental visit); well, that day I was prepared for anything and was excited about everything. If a few minutes of discomfort was part of the process to become pregnant, then I was certainly down for it.

I had taken a month away from my practice so that I could focus all my energy on the process and be at my best to become pregnant without the distractions or pressure of work. This decision was a relatively easy one, particularly because I had a couple of weeks of vacation that I had accumulated. I also did not want the stress of my job to interfere with my goal. I could not envision going through the IVF cycle and working at the same time. I did not want to take any chances. I was going forward with my entire focus on becoming pregnant. I would do whatever it took to ensure my mind, body, and soul were aligned, rested, and at their very best for the whole process. Part of ensuring being at my best was also undergoing alternative holistic health treatments. I opted for acupuncture, a traditional Chinese medicine modality.

I had preconceived notions about acupuncture before I tried it for the first time. To be honest, I never imagined I would try it. The thought of lying still with a bunch of needles stuck in various parts of my body did not appeal to me. It sounded very unpleasant, and the visual certainly didn't seem attractive. I knew that acupuncture was used alone or in combination with conventional therapies to treat a number of conditions, including chronic pain and stress management. However, I had no idea that it was also used to help those experiencing infertility or that it was possible and recommended to receive acupuncture before and during assisted reproduction. Despite my initial reluctance to try it, I thought I had nothing to lose. So, I decided I'd give it a try, and I wouldn't have to go a second time if I didn't want to. The first time was nerve-wracking. I am known to have trouble relaxing during massages—it takes a lot for me to feel comfortable enough to slow down my mind and be in the moment. I didn't particularly enjoy the feeling of the acupuncture needles being inserted into my head and parts of my ears. But as I focused less on the needles and more on slowing my breath and my mind, I began to relax. After the appointment, I noticed that I felt pretty good. I decided to return a week later. That session was unlike the first. I didn't really notice the needles being inserted, and I relaxed to the point that I fell asleep for a few minutes. After the session, I felt terrific. I continued receiving acupuncture regularly throughout that first IVF cycle, and I believe it helped me.

As we moved through the process, I imagined a viable embryo. I imagined the embryo implanting into my uterus, growing and becoming a fetus and finally, a baby. It might sound a little silly, but I was visualizing what I wanted in stages and in great detail. I was visualizing it from a place of knowing and calm. I believed that it was happening. My desire was coming true.

There were four viable embryos from this first cycle. We made the decision to transfer two of them into my uterus and to freeze the remaining two. The chances of becoming pregnant increase with the number of embryos that are transferred. The greater the number transferred, the greater the chance of successful implantation in the uterine wall. To a certain degree this explanation is simplified, as there are other factors at play as well, but generally speaking, your chances of becoming pregnant increase when more than one embryo is transferred. Your chances of having a multiple pregnancy—twins or other multiples—also increase because it is possible for more than one embryo to implant and to develop successfully. We understood this chance and welcomed the opportunity to have twins.

I approached the experience and embraced each stage of the process with an expansive and open heart and love. I was happy. I was excited. I looked forward to my daily appointments at the clinic. After the embryo transfer, I kept envisioning an embryo implanting into my uterus. It might sound odd, but it's true. I was most certainly in a mindset conducive to successful implantation. When I returned to work, I felt at peace and hopeful that good news was on its way. A few days after my return to the office, I called the IVF clinic to inquire about my bloodwork. I'll never forget the voice and words of the nurse on the other end of the line: "Let's see . . . it's positive, and your hCG levels are great." I hung up the phone and jumped for joy. Literally. And then went into a meeting. To this day, I don't know how long the meeting lasted or what it was about. The next few weeks were a time of cautious optimism.

Our joy was cruelly brief.

I remember the ultrasound appointment like it was yesterday. As the technician moved the internal ultrasound wand around my uterus to locate the heartbeat, there was nothing but the sound of my nervous breathing. The sound of my breath was pure anguish. And the words that followed left me feeling gutted: "I'm so sorry." My breath caught in my throat, and I closed my eyes tightly. I felt as if I had been struck through the heart. It was over. Just like that. By the time I had reached the tiny room down the hall to change back into my clothes, I was desperate to sit down again. I held my face in my hands while I wept uncontrollably.

How can one be in the euphoria of pregnancy one moment and in the despair of emptiness the next? How could it be over before it had a chance to truly begin?

A few minutes later, I was sitting in a small office and staring at the gray floor while one of the doctors on the IVF team explained "what happens next." I would need to return to the clinic in a few days to have further tests to confirm whether I had miscarried, as it was possible (but, he stressed, unlikely) that a heartbeat would be detected at that time. I did as I was told. I returned home to wait in a numb state of limbo. I believed that I had miscarried, and I was waiting for confirmation of the most devastating news I had ever received by that time in my life. I returned to the clinic. Nothing had changed. My world was just as it was. Empty. I was given a prescription for something to expedite the pregnancy loss process (the shedding of the uterine wall). I filled my prescription, returned to my home, and awaited the inevitable.

I knew nothing about the ordeal I was about to go through. For the first time in months, I did not have to wait at all. The medication did what it was supposed to do. And nothing could have prepared me for it. The pain was ferocious, and the bleeding was equally so. I thought that I had developed a tolerance for cramping because I had always had painful periods. Well, this time was different. And the bleeding? I recall it lasted for at least ten days. Mourning the loss of a pregnancy while in this physical state was excruciating. It was heartbreaking.

About three months following the miscarriage, we made a decision about the remaining two viable embryos that we had frozen during our first cycle. We decided to try again. That cycle was ultimately delayed in order to await a more optimal state of my follicles and uterine wall. When we were given the go-ahead a month later, we had both embryos transferred. However, that cycle did not result in a pregnancy. I felt incredibly sad and empty.

I would say that it was at this point when my fertility journey began to change from one fueled by hope and faith to one mired in fear and urgency.

If we tried again, I wouldn't get pregnant.
If we tried again and I somehow managed to get pregnant, I would miscarry.
I had already miscarried, so what made me think I could do it successfully?
My track record was terrible; who was I to think I could pull this off?
What was I doing, putting myself and my husband through this procedure again? What was the point?

I was plagued by limiting beliefs and visions of catastrophic outcomes. My vibration, my energy, was not conducive to manifesting my desired outcome of having a baby. But we longed to be parents. We could not ignore what our hearts so desperately wanted. We decided to try again.

For our third IVF cycle, I made the difficult decision to take a three-month leave from my law practice. I was fortunate to have worked at a firm of several lawyers because I could disperse my files to other lawyers to carry in my absence. I was so grateful to have this opportunity.

It is not lost on me that many lawyers, particularly those who are sole practitioners, would not have even been able to consider transferring work as an option.

This IVF cycle was a full cycle, as we did not have any frozen embryos remaining, which meant that we had to undergo the entire process to suppress and then stimulate ovulation, to conduct the egg retrieval, fertilization, the creation of the viable embryo(s) and then finally, the embryo transfer into my uterus. We had four viable embryos from this cycle.

After consulting with my doctor, we decided to transfer *three embryos*, more than we had transferred in the first two cycles. The transfer of three meant that it was possible for more than one embryo to implant, meaning that there was a chance we may not only have twins, but possibly triplets. Multiples are at greater risk of having health problems, something we had to consider as well. The decision to transfer three embryos was not made lightly. Our thoughts of a possible multiple birth were short-lived, however, because this third cycle did not result in pregnancy.

Everything changed with this outcome.

This was it. This was my reckoning. I was done. The outcome of this third cycle signaled the end of our assisted reproduction journey. I was devastated. I was emotionally spent and numb and did not know how I would ever recover and piece my life together again. I felt utterly defeated. I would never know what it was like to be pregnant again, and I would never know what it was like to carry a baby to term, to give birth, and to raise a child.

A few days after learning the results of that cycle, we talked about what was next and made the decision not to make any decisions about our remaining embryo for the time being. We desperately needed a respite from the assisted reproduction process. We were tired—so tired. More importantly, we needed to heal. We needed to replenish ourselves emotionally, mentally, and physically.

And then, in a matter of two weeks, my husband experienced the most devastating loss of his lifetime. The sudden loss of *both* of his parents and his childhood home to a fire was a blow like no other.

It is true what they say: life can change in an instant. In just two weeks, I went from being drained and numb from our third assisted reproduction attempt to a wife desperately trying to help her husband survive the incomprehensible deaths of his parents while also feeling the loss of two wonderful people I loved dearly and who had become second parents to me.

To be struck with this unimaginable event at a time in our lives when we had experienced the pain of infertility and pregnancy loss, years of it, seemed unbelievably cruel. It felt like fate was playing a tortuous game with us. I remember questioning my religion and everything I believed in. I remember being extremely sad and angry but also doing everything to find the strength to support my husband to ensure that he got the help that he needed.

What I did not do was acknowledge that I, too, was experiencing loss. While I ensured that Jeff received the support that he needed, I did not take any steps to deal with my own grief. Instead, I did what I had learned to do well—I buried it in my work. I buried my grief and muted it. Subconsciously, I decided that it mattered less. Perhaps I did not truly understand that I was grieving as well, albeit not in the same way that my husband was, and that I really needed to acknowledge it and allow myself to feel it and go through it.

The next several months were about ensuring my husband received the mental health support he required and addressing and managing legal responsibilities. It was truly about helping my husband through the most painful event in his lifetime. We tried to move forward as best as we could. But despite it all, although perhaps less visible than before, our desire to become parents remained omnipresent.

We soon realized that it was time to consider another option. My in-laws had adopted two children: my husband, then his sister two years later (they are not biologically related). Both were adopted as infants, and both were told about their birth and adoption stories as young children. Jeff and I had talked about whether adoption would be a possibility for our family when we were going through our struggles, and we decided that if we could not have biological children, we would adopt.

Adoption is a very involved process with a lot of "homework." There are many decisions and steps involved, particularly at the outset of the process. Would the adoption be domestic, meaning that our search for a child would be limited to the jurisdiction of Canada, or would the adoption be international? Were we open to adopting an older child or only an infant? Would we consider sibling adoption, meaning adopting two children who are siblings? Were we open to considering children with physical or mental challenges? Were we willing to adopt a child of any age? There was *a lot* to consider. In many ways, it was overwhelming. We consulted with an adoption practitioner, completed our home study, took the required weekend course, prepared our adoption profile (a detailed narrative, or letter to a prospective birth mother, about our lives and journey), and then waited.

We were no strangers to the waiting game.

We had waited, from month to month, for me to miss a period and to see a positive pregnancy test.

We had waited to see a specialist to determine what was "wrong."

We had waited to each undergo testing, some of which was far from pleasant.

We had waited after I had been poked and prodded and "ultrasounded" to be told our result and, if "positive," my human chorionic gonadotropin (or hCG) levels.

We had waited to have the ultrasound to detect the fetus's heartbeat.

We had waited for my body to complete the process of loss and to shed its uterine wall.

And now, we were waiting for a birth mother to read our profile, connect with our story, and choose us to become parents of her child.

Writing your adoption profile or letter is a strange exercise. Essentially, you and your partner are making a pitch to a potential birth mother about why you are the ones she should choose to parent her biological child. I was initially uncomfortable with the idea of writing about myself and my husband in this way; it almost felt like a sales pitch (actually, that is exactly what it felt like, initially). I can't tell you how many rewrites we went through. There were several. And the writing piece was not the half of it. You see, the profile or letter has evolved to become a hardcover book of text and photographs. So, if the exercise of writing felt "salesy," can you imagine how it felt to put together a catalogue, if you will, of the would-be parents, their home, and things about their life? It felt really bizarre. But we understood its importance. And soon enough, we started to think of it as less of a sales strategy and more of an opportunity to connect with a woman who was on her own unique and undoubtedly challenging journey, one that we would never be able to understand. We eventually got a little caught up in the excitement of creating something that would speak to a birth mother in such a way that we would become adoptive parents—that we would have a child.

We created an impressive profile book. You could say we let our creativity and our hearts run wild and help us unfold our desires in a way that was authentic, simple, and beautiful. And communicating authentically was very important to us.

And then we waited.

And waited.

And waited.

One month turned into two. Two months turned into four. Four months turned into eight. And so on.

While we waited "to be chosen," I created an entire script of why we were not "being chosen." Some of the storyline went like this:

We were *too old* to be parents.

We were *too educated*.

We seemed *entitled*.

We *did not have enough experience* with children.

My job was *too demanding*.

Our child would have *only one set of grandparents*, as he or she would never know his paternal grandparents.

Jeff had recently experienced the traumatic loss of his parents and perhaps *was not emotionally ready* for parenthood?

On and on the narrative spun.

As if this stress were not enough, I started paying closer attention to statistics. There were fewer and fewer infant children available for adoption, and the decline in the availability of infants and young children was even more prevalent in the case of domestic adoptions.

These statistics were no secret, as they were repeatedly explained to us in the literature we read, in the information provided by our practitioner, and in the course we were required to complete. I was thankful for the transparency and honesty. However, I began fixating on these statistics, and they soon began to control my thoughts and feelings.

The comments of well-intentioned family and friends also began to affect my mindset about what I was doing:

"How will you know the baby's health history?"

"Aren't you worried about unknown health problems?"

"What if the child develops something you did not expect?"

"What if you don't bond with the baby?"

"What if your child turns away from you when they learn they are adopted?"

"What if you encounter difficulties with the birth mother in the future?"

"What if the birth mother changes her mind?"

Although I rationally understood that there is truly never any certainty when it comes to health and expectations, including the health of your biological child, and although I was able to put aside some of these comments, the ones about the birth mother changing her mind and reconsidering her decision struck a nerve, and to be honest, they did worry me to some extent.

For the most part, however, we remained calm and optimistic. We understood that the adoption process was a long game and expecting quick results was unrealistic. We were also aware of the legal steps and requirements that had to be completed for the process to become formalized. Since I was a lawyer and therefore somewhat familiar with what was required to legalize the adoption, that piece did not really concern me. It was the waiting and the uncertainty that was difficult.

We stayed the course and did whatever was needed to be blessed with being chosen to become the parents of a child—our child.

I wanted to believe that our baby would find us. That we would be parents, timelines, statistics, and all logic be damned. I realized that there is power within the wait, strength in the anguish and loss, and blessings that have yet to be uncovered. I felt like our time was coming . . . and that all of what we had been through wouldn't have been for naught.

Pause, reflect, lean in

- *Think back to a time in your life when you navigated something challenging or traumatic. What did you feel at the time?*
- *Looking back, can you identify your moments of strength, grace, and compassion that shined through?*
- *What would you tell yourself in hindsight?*

Chapter Eleven

Something Had to Give

When we made the decision to adopt, we were releasing a part of us that longed to be biological parents and embracing the possibility that we would become parents a different way. We were letting go of the all-consuming desire to conceive a baby and welcoming the birth of a child through our hearts.

I don't really know whether we were conscious of this shift happening, but I really believe that it was present because otherwise we would not have been able to complete the requirements and follow through with the responsibilities that were required to adopt a child.

While we waited, we made the decision to attempt IVF one final time. We had a single frozen embryo, and we arranged for the transfer.

In hindsight, the decision to do it was made from a different place: that of obligation and fear. We did not feel good about leaving our embryo in a laboratory for an unknown period of time. Something did not feel "right" about that. We were afraid. The loss of Jeff's parents and the difficult year that followed also made this time less than ideal to make a huge decision and proceed with something as involved as assisted reproduction. In hindsight, although my head had made the decision to transfer our last embryo, my heart was not entirely in it.

My internal state was very different this time, and by different, I don't mean better. I was incredibly anxious leading up to the day of the embryo transfer procedure. I shared my anxiety with my fertility doctor, and he prescribed a very mild dose of Atavan so that I could take it just before the procedure.

While the nurse helped me into the stirrups and adjusted me on the examination table, I felt a subtle snap in my lower back. It concerned me for a moment, but I put it out of my mind until after the transfer was completed and Jeff and I were alone in the room. "I felt something strange in my back just before the transfer," I said to my husband. Although he looked concerned, he gently told me not to worry and to focus on relaxing. A few minutes later, we were on our way home. Instead of spending the rest of the day resting and remaining calm, I was a bundle of nerves. I did not like how I felt emotionally or physically. As the day went on, I felt increasing discomfort and then pain. The day following the transfer, I was in excruciating pain and had trouble sitting and walking. I was terrified that the embryo would not implant in my uterus while my body was in this stressful state. But I did what I thought I needed to do. I refused to take anything for the pain because I did not want to take any risks while I waited to find out if I was pregnant.

Did I mention that the blood test to confirm whether there is a pregnancy occurs twelve to fourteen days following the embryo transfer?

I was plagued with doubt about the success of the procedure but also afraid to do anything to compromise a possible pregnancy. This duality provoked extreme anxiety, and these feelings of anxiety were compounded by the extreme and chronic pain I was experiencing physically. In short, I was a mess.

How I got to the clinic for my blood work is a mystery. By that time, I would have been horizontal for much of the day. I actually don't remember how I got there. Jeff very likely drove me, but I have no memory of it.

When I received my results and learned what I had already known deep in my heart, that the cycle had not been successful and I was not pregnant, I finally saw my family doctor. She was very concerned about the severity of my pain and also stunned by the fact that I had waited two weeks to see her. She scheduled an urgent MRI, which revealed that I had herniated two discs in my lower spine that were compressing a nerve. The next several months were extremely difficult. I remember lying on the floor of my office while taking phone calls and dictating correspondence and stopping more than once during my drive to work to get out of the car (when I was able to go to the office). I was treated by a chiropractor for two years, initially several times a week and ultimately weekly and biweekly. It was not easy to do while running a busy law practice. Looking back, I do not know how I survived or made it through each day.

I was living on autopilot, living each day by going through the motions but doing so while in some degree of pain or discomfort. The next year or so was the most physically and emotionally difficult part of navigating my career as a lawyer. I fell completely and utterly apart.

As someone who planned almost every moment of her life and remained consistent with her plans, putting one foot in front of the other, moving forward and succeeding, I felt lost. Going through infertility made me feel powerless, a feeling that I had not really known before. I wanted to do whatever I could to become a mother. I *was* doing whatever I could. But it was not working. It made me feel like I wasn't doing enough, that I wasn't enough. And then my back injury and the physical and emotional challenges that followed contributed to my feelings of low worth and despair. All of this was extremely defeating and upsetting.

However, while navigating this journey, I discovered parts of me that I never knew were there. Parts of me that were stronger than I ever imagined. Things that I would have deemed scary or too challenging or risky or painful before this experience were now viewed as essential and necessary, and possible. I evolved. I grew. I was no longer the same woman who walked into this beautiful and life-changing storm. I shed parts of me that I no longer needed. I became softer and harder, at the same time. I became different.

Four IVF cycles, the loss of loved ones, recurrent pregnancy loss, an unsuccessful adoption journey: the culmination of these events changed me profoundly. How could it not?

It was life changing for Jeff too.

We easily forget that it is not only women who live this journey. Their partners also experience loss and pain, but they typically hide it well, consciously or not. After all, men[3] are *supposed* to be the strong ones, the ones who support their partners, the ones who take care of them, the ones who are not allowed to be "weak" or acknowledge their own pain.

When a couple is going through assisted reproduction, the focus of the medical professionals, family, friends, and support network seems to be on the woman, as she is the one who undergoes the invasive process of having injections, blood tests, ultrasounds, and so on. But the partners of those women are also living the experience, and although they may be doing so differently, their experience remains an emotionally heavy journey as well because they are entrusted with the duty of being a supportive partner while processing their own experience, likely without ever admitting to others (or even themselves) that they are hurting and experiencing a journey themselves.

Infertility was the first huge life challenge that Jeff and I had to navigate together. I was so focused on myself, I doubt I gave Jeff the space to feel comfortable to experience and express that he was struggling too, and that it was not only fine for him to have this struggle,

____

3 Although the terms I am using refer to heterosexual couples, LBGTQ2S+ pursue assisted reproduction as well. My terminology is not meant to be restrictive or insulting; I am using the terms "men" and "women" for ease, and they are not intended to be insensitive or to exclude.

but it was *necessary* to his emotional health and well-being. I believe it is important to communicate this information with your partner and to never assume that they already know or understand it simply because they see you going through it. At the risk of overgeneralizing, men have been conditioned by their upbringing, society, culture, or all three that they need to be strong and stoic. Furthermore, being strong and expressing pain and emotion are mutually exclusive. Your partner is likely so worried about how you are doing through the process that he isn't even realizing or understanding the depths of what he is experiencing and that it is also *his* journey. It may not be the same journey and the same experience that you are having, but your partner is living his journey, and his experience matters just as much.

Jeff wanted to be a dad as much as I wanted to be a mom. He may not have talked about it as frequently or as openly as I did, but that did not minimize his desire to be a father. I saw it in his interactions with our nieces and nephews and on his face with each failed IVF cycle and pregnancy loss. Although I was supportive of my husband and knew he was struggling as well, I did not have the awareness then of the nature of his journey or how he was navigating it. In some ways, I suppose it was not possible for me to understand it at the time while I was in the midst of the journey myself. However, in hindsight, I do recognize that I could have been more present for Jeff and given him the grace and space to feel and live through whatever that looked like for him. More than anything, I could have acknowledged that the experience was truly *ours*.

Jeff and I shared many moments of tenderness and love, and we also shed many tears together. We were each living and experiencing our own unique individual journeys while also going through this very challenging part of our lives together. It wasn't just the bond of marriage that connected us to each other, it was much more. Our fertility journey was a difficult part of our lives together, but it was also a part that brought us closer and solidified our bond. It is these collective experiences that have given us a close understanding of ourselves and each other. It has allowed us to show up with enormous grace, kindness, and compassion for ourselves, each other, our son, and, of course, anyone with whom we interact.

Pause, reflect, lean in

- *Can you recall a time you navigated a challenging situation together with a partner, a friend, or family member?*
- *How did you feel? Do you know their experience?*
- *Could you have approached things differently?*
- *What shifted within you? How did these experiences help you grow as individuals, as partners, as a family, or even as a team?*
- *What would you tell yourself, in hindsight?*
- *What would you share with them, in hindsight?*

Chapter Twelve

Surrendering Control and Embracing Abundance

As Jeff and I began to heal together through our support and love for each other, our hearts began to expand with gratitude. Then one day, we made the decision to grow our family in a different way. We are both dog lovers and had had dogs growing up. Having a pup was part of our "one day" or "after we have kids" plan. Well, we shook up that plan and decided it was time to share our family with a dog. One sunny August day, we welcomed a nine-week-old beautiful golden retriever into our home, and his presence reignited a wonderful light of gratitude and joy that had been dimmed for a long time. We began to live in the beautiful moment rather than being fixated on the future and on our longing for a child.

I know what you must be thinking: *Who gets a golden retriever when they are trying to recover from a serious back injury?*

It's a fair question. When we brought Dylan home, he was about fifteen pounds, but he quickly grew to thirty pounds and then fifty pounds and then seventy pounds. He's been between seventy-four and seventy-eight pounds for the last few years. I realized soon enough that I would not be able to walk Dylan alone, at least not for the first year. I could not risk frustrating my injury and causing more permanent damage. When my back strengthened and I became more confident in my ability, I had trouble controlling Dylan on walks, but not because of his behavior toward other dogs and people (he is incredibly friendly and gentle, either rolling onto his back for a belly rub or sitting on people's feet until they pet him or give him a treat). As a larger breed, he is strong and pulls on the leash. He has also had a bad habit of eating twigs, sticks, and pinecones since he was a little puppy. When my husband firmly commands "drop it," Dylan almost always does so, but when I voice the command, he only seems to ingest what he's put into his mouth faster. He's now eight, and although this behavior has subsided to an extent, we've come to terms with the fact that it is what it is, and Dylan is not going to outgrow it.

Dylan was like the secret ingredient that was sprinkled onto our lives and changed us forever. He brought so much unconditional love into our home. Caring for a dog is therapeutic and joyful. Having another living being to love and care for is incredibly gratifying. It was the first time in years that we felt complete and truly happy.

Sharing the love that I had in my heart with my dog caused a profound shift in my mindset. The distorted and cracked lens through which I viewed my life became clear and focused. I started to appreciate *who I was* and *what I had*—my husband, my family, my friends, my home, my career, my health, *and my beautiful dog*—instead of longing for what I thought was missing. I became more engaged in my daily activities, sought out new experiences, and began to feel like a full participant in my life. I became grounded in the present and the beauty of enjoying the small things. The feelings of resentment and despair melted away, and I learned to let go and trust that things were unfolding exactly as they were meant to unfold.

We updated our adoption profile letter (the book) to include our pup. He was, after all, a member of our family, and it was important that we were transparent with anyone who would be considering us as adoptive parents to their biological child. We were still hoping to adopt an infant or toddler, and we prayed that our story would resonate with someone so we would be united with a child. But for the first time, we realized that we would be fine if we did not adopt. We would be okay. Did we still want a child, did we still want to be parents? Yes. However, we were no longer *attached to the* outcome. Our life was no longer defined by longing, by yearning, by waiting for completion. *We were already complete, and so we began to let go.*

I felt a closeness to my husband that I had not felt in years. Our conversations effortlessly returned to our interests and what we had in common rather than what we thought we lacked. We discussed books, music, current events, causes that we believed in, our careers— everything that brought connection and joy. We laughed—a lot. The sound of laughter and spontaneous expression filled our home. I was reconnecting with my husband, and we were bonding with the new member of our family. For the first time in years, planning our intimacy around my ovulation cycle, discussing when to schedule our next IVF cycle, weighing our adoption route options, and updating our adoption profile were things that were simply not on the agenda.

For the first time in years, there was no agenda.

I still struggled with my back issues, which made managing a demanding law practice challenging. But truth be told, it was more than my injured back that was causing a shift. Looking back, I really don't understand how I did it—managing a career in family law, dealing with infertility, undergoing IVF four times, trying to adopt, losing Jeff's parents suddenly, and sustaining a back injury—all in the span of less than four years. I suppose it was strength. But strength or not, I knew it was impossible to continue on this path. I decided to take a six-month sabbatical from my practice to give myself time to heal emotionally, to get physically stronger, and to decide whether I wanted to return to my career or pursue something else.

I was glad to be taking time for myself, but I was also quite apprehensive about being away from my firm. *A sabbatical—what would people think? Would they think that something was wrong? Would they think that something was wrong with me? Would they think I could no longer handle family law? Would they think I was taking time away to try to have a baby again?* I worried about the conclusions the family law bar would draw—that I was burnt out, and that I was no longer cut out to practice. I feared the judgment of my peers, even though I knew that at their core these fears were baseless. Ultimately, I knew that taking the sabbatical was the right decision *for me.*

Well, when I announced that I would be going on sabbatical, the response I got from my peers and colleagues was supportive. People congratulated me, they wished me well, they told me they wished they could do what I was doing. They respected my decision and were happy for me. And then I received the most unexpected but welcomed gift two days into my six-month break.

My period was late.
My period is never late.

I was shopping at a mall when I got the impulse to purchase a home pregnancy test. I was on such a nervous high as I walked out of the store, my tote bag under my arm and within it a test that was about to tell me if I had a baby growing inside of me. I didn't even wait until I got home—I took the test in the food court restroom. I remember my hands shaking and my stomach doing backflips. I not only had butterflies, I had butterflies on steroids. I was nearly dizzy with excitement and nerves. Imagine my reaction when I saw "Yes+" on the pregnancy stick. *I was pregnant?!* It was the first time we had conceived naturally. We had been rekindling our relationship, but we were not trying to get pregnant. I was stunned and overjoyed. *I was pregnant!* Doubting my ability to vocalize the result to Jeff and fearing that *I* would think I had imagined all of it before I could even speak to him, I took a photograph of the positive result. I'll never forget the look on Jeff's face. He was as stunned and ecstatic as I was.

The next while was a dream-like trance of excitement and worry. I had experienced one miscarriage, and I was afraid it would happen again. It did. I miscarried at about eight weeks. The ordeal was shorter this time but more painful. When I first started bleeding, the pain was indescribable. I came very close to fainting from the intensity. A short while later, we were sitting in the hospital emergency room. As someone who lived with painful periods, I was used to having bad cramps, and Jeff often joked that I had the highest pain threshold of anyone he knew. However, this pain was something different altogether. I sat in the emergency room, doubled over for close to two hours without seeing a doctor before going home.

An appointment with my ob-gyn confirmed that I had miscarried, and although it was not possible to determine with certainty, the pregnancy had likely been ectopic.[4] Did this news make the loss easier to understand and accept? Not really. It was the loss of a pregnancy. It was the loss of my pregnancy. This second miscarriage was devastating. I mourned just as I had mourned my first pregnancy four years earlier, but I came through the experience with what I now understand to be resilience and with a resolve to continue on the path that I was on, one of gratitude and love for my family and life.

---

4 An ectopic pregnancy is when a fertilized egg implants and grows outside of the main cavity of the uterus, commonly in the fallopian tube. An ectopic pregnancy is fatal to the fetus, as it cannot survive outside of the uterus.

I slowly developed a semblance of a routine and experienced a state that I best describe as equilibrium. Although I wasn't working, I kept myself busy with doing things I enjoyed and putting my energy into household projects that I had postponed for years. I was reading, listening to a ton of music, going for daily walks with my dog, eating better, seeing my chiropractor regularly, and implementing the exercises he prescribed for my lower back. The chaos of the previous several years had made way for clarity.

We visited a spa for a long weekend during the summer, and as I typically do, I packed a couple of books to enjoy by the pool. One of these was Michael A. Singer's *The Untethered Soul: The Journey Beyond Yourself.* It was a spontaneous purchase because of its calming aquamarine and gray cover with an image of a horse running freely on a beach. Not only did the book exceed my expectations, but it also gave me beautiful insights and instruction that helped me further along the path of transformation that was taking place in my subconscious. I hadn't looked at Singer's book in years until I was about to start writing this book, and I was surprised by how much of it I had underlined and dog-eared. It had obviously made a significant impression. Here is one of the passages I had marked:

So there are two ways you can live: you can devote your life to staying in your comfort zone, or you can work on your freedom. In other words, you can devote your whole life to the process of making sure everything fits within your limited model, or you can devote your life to freeing yourself from the limits of your model.

Whoa.

I suggest you read that paragraph a couple more times to allow its meaning to really sink in.

Can you feel its message?

Something was happening to me and through me. I was finally living from the *inside out* rather than from the *outside in*. I was abandoning my limited model of seeing myself surrounded by lack. I was stepping into freedom and embracing abundance.

And then my beautiful and wise mother wrote me a letter.

My husband and I had gone out to lunch with my parents, and at the end of the meal, my mother looked at me and placed a folded piece of paper into my hands.

It was a heartfelt, handwritten letter that not only reaffirmed my mother's unconditional and unwavering love for her daughter and the woman I had become but also *reaffirmed in me* the awareness that I was not on the frequency to understand and receive because I was seeing my goal of becoming a mother through the lens of loss and lack. Quite simply, it reaffirmed for me *my knowing*—that I was loved no less because I did not have a child, that I was loved unconditionally by my husband, by our dog, and that we were truly a family. It reaffirmed for me that my parents' love for me was constant whether or not I became a mother. Finally, it crystallized *my knowing* that I would have a child if, when, and how it was meant to happen, *and I was okay with all of it; in fact, I was more than okay.*

I had spent years molded by circumstance, living with longing, and trying to control *if, when,* and *how* I would become a mother. For the first time in years, I had clarity about what I needed, and what I needed was to relinquish control of my fertility journey and my life as a whole. For the first time in years, I was able to be fully present. Lawyers chronically fail at being present because they are almost always anticipating problems, claims and losses, structuring and strategizing, and creating safeguards to protect their clients. Isn't that what contracts do? They define and outline mutual expectations and rights and obligations so that the parties have certainty, or at least as much certainty as possible when a particular event occurs. I was not only a planner and worrier and perfectionist by nature for much of my life (the process likely began in utero), but I was also in a two-decade–long career where I planned, worried, and perfected every day. I lived it.

You can therefore imagine how huge this shift was for me!

I was no longer consumed by the future, nor was I shackled by my past struggles and experiences. The present took on more meaning and importance than it probably ever has in my adult life. I began living in the now, and it became habitual and then natural. I enjoyed the simplicity of things that I had ignored for years and embraced the things that gave me joy: long walks in nature, day trips outside of the city, visits to the spa, leisurely lunches, jazz concerts, movie nights, cottage stays, time with my parents and siblings reminiscing about growing up as a family, time catching up with friends, daily walks with my dog, eating healthier, getting regular exercise, making improvements to my home, cooking (some) meals—I eased into it all and found a beautiful rhythm.

I let go of my need for control and trusted that things were unfolding the way that they were meant to unfold. I surrendered to a larger power, call it the Universe, God, whatever word works for you and helps you to understand. I leaned in, proverbial white flag raised high, and I surrendered. I cut away the chains that tethered me to the bonds of anguish and despair, *and I freed myself.*

As the end of my sabbatical drew near, we left our pup in the care of my parents and traveled to San Francisco and Monterey, California, for a week in September during which time we attended the Monterey Jazz Festival. It had been our dream (and an item on our bucket list) to attend this jazz festival. We had talked about it for a number of years as something we would do "one day." When we made the spontaneous decision to purchase our tickets less than two weeks before our departure date, we were incredibly excited. The timing of the trip coincided with our twelfth wedding anniversary. This adventure was exactly what we needed, and for me, it was probably one of our most memorable trips. This California vacation was the first time in a very, very long time where I remember being present for every beautiful moment. Whether it was taking the trolley down to the waterfront in San Francisco, walking along the beach and enjoying a leisurely lunch in Carmel-by-the-Sea, enjoying lobster dinner while watching the sea lions in Monterey, or spending an entire day watching and listening to the likes of Herbie Hancock, Cécile McLorin Salvant, and Marcus Miller perform at the open-air jazz festival, I was fully present and in the beauty and flow of the *now*.

We returned home refreshed and happy. A few days later, and just two days before my scheduled return to my firm, I realized that my period was late—*several days late*. The strange thing was that I had not noticed right away. It did not even enter my mind. I took a home pregnancy test and the result was *positive*. We were beyond elated and stunned. Even in my state of euphoria, I calmly and cautiously contacted my obstetrician, who was almost as surprised to hear back from me with pregnancy news less than six months from the last time I saw him, and I arranged to have an ultrasound.

"There it is." The technician's words were quiet but unmistakable. I was lying on my back with my eyes closed and my hands held together while undergoing an internal ultrasound. The technician had detected a heartbeat. *There was a fetus with a beating heart inside of me.* I closed my eyes, thanked God, and was overwhelmed with love and gratitude. I left the appointment feeling as if I were floating.

While we had been in Monterey, I was not really looking forward to the end of our trip and our return home. I was apprehensive after being away from the practice of law for six months. However, I now welcomed it with open arms. I was ready. I made the decision to wait until I was three months along before sharing the news with those outside of my family. Holding this secret, my joy, close, within my heart, was amazing. Perhaps my face let on more than I thought, and others were aware of more than I knew. I couldn't stop smiling, even during those difficult meetings or court appearances. Was I nervous? Of course. Having experienced recurrent pregnancy loss, an element of fear and worry forever lurks beneath the surface. The difference, however, was that I was not consumed with nerves and worry. The next several months of my fertility path were not paved with fear but with peace, trust, and knowing—knowing that everything would work out the way that it was supposed to and that I would be fine and my baby would be fine. My dominant state was no longer one of fear and lack, it was one of peace and abundance.

An appointment with my obstetrician when I was further along in my pregnancy forever solidified the enormity of what was happening. I will never forget the *sound* of my little one's heartbeat. The sound filled my ears, my heart, my entire being. I was euphoric but also calm and at peace. It was real. I wasn't dreaming. I was fully awake. I was having a baby.

A baby.
My baby. Our baby.
I was going to be a mother.

I was forever changed. Life would never be the same again. *So, this is what it feels like when your deepest held desire comes to fruition. Thank you, thank you, and thank you.*

Pause, reflect, lean in

- *Can you recall a moment when your deepest desire(s) came true?*

- *How did you welcome it? Did you celebrate, lean into self-trust and gratitude?*

- *Or did you wait for the other shoe to drop?*

- *What would it feel like to fully surrender into each moment, knowing that the Universe is always working in your favor?*

- *Write a letter to yourself welcoming all your desires, all the ways in which you've grown, evolved, expanded. Bless it and release any attachments to outcomes. Open it after ninety days, six months, or even a whole year.*

Chapter Thirteen

Pregnancy and Postpartum

Well, we did it. I did it. My body did it. I had a full-term, uneventful pregnancy. I was probably the calmest I had been in years. I felt physically and emotionally well, for the most part. My mind was clear, and I slept better in my first trimester than I had in most of my adult life.

Because I conceived at forty-one, I underwent genetic testing and was closely monitored throughout. We chose to find out the sex, but I already knew I was having a boy before my doctor disclosed it. I don't know why, but each time I pictured my child, I pictured a boy. My husband and I had no preference, we just prayed for a healthy baby, girl or boy. But when I spoke and sang to my unborn child, when I rubbed my belly, when I imagined holding my child in my arms, I pictured a blond, gray-eyed boy. I am not blonde (my dark brown hair is often mistaken for black), and neither is my husband. But when I pictured my child, I pictured a blond-haired boy. My son.

My son was with me as I went about my day, as I talked on the phone, as I met with a client, and as I conducted a matter in court. He was with me as I read the literature on pregnancy and a baby's first year, as I purchased items to prepare for his arrival, as I decorated his nursery, as I sang to him, and as I spoke to him, sharing stories about how much I wanted to be a mom and how much he was already loved.

Throughout my pregnancy, our dog, Dylan, was by my side more than usual, particularly during the last trimester. He would often snuggle beside me, resting his head on my belly. He would look up at me with his intense dark brown eyes, and I would tell him about the baby that was growing inside of me. I would tell him that there would soon be another member of the family who would love him and who he would love too. I believe that dogs have a sense for these things and that Dylan understood that our family would soon grow to four.

I loved being pregnant.

I was consumed.

I felt so different that I expected people to look at me differently, even when I was just beginning to show. Surely, they noticed the changes in me as well.

I felt beautiful, alive, at peace, complete, whole. I would catch glimpses of myself in mirrors and windows and stare at my reflection, getting lost in it. I loved the glow of my skin and the luster and full-ness of my hair. I loved touching and holding my belly. I loved the peacefulness of my thoughts and clear focus of my mind.

I talked to and sang to my unborn child every day. I knew him before I even saw his face. I loved him before I felt his skin, knew his scent, and heard his cries.

I loved to feel the growing and stretching of my abdomen. The physical changes and sensations of pregnancy are strange to describe, that tightness and pressure, almost like a feeling of being full all the time. I remember it made taking deep breaths a challenge.

I did not have any morning sickness, and its absence initially worried me ("Is this normal?" I would ask my doctor, my mother). I felt good and slept well during the first two trimesters, but by the third trimester, I was having very painful nightly foot and lower leg cramps. These would wake me (every night and usually repeatedly during the night), and I would have to get out of bed and try to walk (it was not easy) to lessen the cramping. If you've ever suffered from foot and lower leg cramps (at the point where your foot and leg meet), you'll know how uncomfortable the feeling is and how painful it can be.

During my last trimester, I also had what felt like tearing and pull-ing in a small area in the upper right quadrant of my abdomen, a symptom of scarring from gallbladder removal surgery several years before. The discomfort worsened as my abdomen expanded, making even sitting upright difficult. Lying flat on my back was the only way I could get a respite from the discomfort and pain when it was at its worst (and it was daily). I managed by borrowing my boss's couch for twenty minutes a day, sometimes more than once a day, to alleviate the discomfort. It was truly the only way I was able to get through my workday. Aside from these issues, I am grateful that I had a healthy and uneventful pregnancy.

Our son, James, was born in May of 2015. We are both May babies (our birthdays are eight days apart), and we share the astrological sign of Gemini.

I knew that I would be induced as my due date approached, and my doctor arranged a bulb induction procedure to dilate my cervix the evening before my scheduled delivery. The procedure took longer than I expected and was extremely uncomfortable. I left the hospital with a balloon and catheter contraption inside of my vagina and taped to the inside of my thigh. I had some bleeding following the procedure and felt the blood running down the inside of my thigh as I walked out of the hospital. I remember turning to my mother who was with me and saying, "I don't think I can do this, Mom." She grabbed my hand, squeezed it, told me that I was incredibly strong and that she would be with me every step of the way.

I didn't get a lot of sleep that night. I was less worried about what was to come the following day and more uncomfortable and worried about what was going on inside of me. We arrived at the hospital at 8:00 the following morning. My water broke (to be accurate, the doctor broke my water, it didn't happen on its own) an hour or so later. I was given an epidural at some point. I was administered medication to facilitate contractions. I remember pushing for several hours. At one point, I developed a low-grade fever. My husband tried to stay calm, but I could see the worry in his eyes. My mother was wearing out the carpet with her pacing. Finally, at 11:54 p.m., my son came into the world, his howls filling the room and my stunned ears, and perhaps foreshadowing what was to come.

Holding him in my arms was an indescribable feeling. I had waited for this moment for an eternity. I looked at my baby's face and the emotions washed over me. I was in love, and I was incredibly grateful. I was finally a mother.

However, like many things in life, the experience of first-time motherhood was complicated. Although I wanted to become a mother with every fiber of my being, I am not going to sugarcoat the complexity and rawness and reality of my personal experience. Becoming a mother, at least in the early days, was certainly not all rainbows and unicorns. Actually, it was nothing like rainbows and unicorns. To be honest, motherhood hit me like a two-by-four.

Going from years of struggling to have a baby, to finally being pregnant, to having a birth experience that you cannot truly prepare yourself for (even if you're a planner like I am), does something to you emotionally. I think that when I was no longer pregnant, I actually felt a loss. I did not understand it then because I did not have the awareness that something was happening to me and what that was. The best way that I can articulate it now is that I missed the euphoria, the calm, the peace, and the fullness of my being that came with pregnancy. I felt complete when I was pregnant. And then I was no longer pregnant. There was a beautiful baby in my arms: I could see his face, hear his breathing and his cries, feel him drinking my milk, and smell his delicious baby scent. *How could I possibly miss being pregnant?* What I now understand is that although I loved my child deeply, the dominant emotions I had in the days and weeks, perhaps even the first few months after giving birth, were emotions of fear, sadness, self-doubt, inadequacy, and even shame, and these emotions and feelings dimmed those of happiness, joy, and peace.

I didn't really expect those hard initial days. No one warned me, not that I really expected them to, as I didn't really ask. The reading I did to prepare myself for the birth and the first year of my child's life seemed to gloss over the hard parts, or perhaps I paid little attention to them. What I thought I prepared myself for was unlike what I experienced. My mom stayed over for about a week (or was it longer?) following the birth. Leading up to the birth, I expected she would be there for a couple of nights as she had done for my sister when she had her first child. Looking back, I am eternally grateful that she stayed with us for as long as she did, as it was a generous gift that she gave me and my family.

When friends and colleagues politely asked to visit, I gently responded, "Sure, that would be wonderful once we get more of a rhythm and routine established," thinking that it was not likely to happen any time soon and being relieved as the thought of anyone witnessing my ineptitude was anxiety inducing.

When I was pregnant and after giving birth, my mother would tell me that the days when we were newborns were the happiest in her life. But I could not relate. *How could something so hard make someone so happy? How could someone be the happiest during something so exhausting and difficult?*

Even though we had always been close, I felt embarrassed and ashamed to talk to my sister whose children were thirteen and ten by then. *What would I say? That I was a fraud? That I wanted to be a mother so much and spent years trying everything to get it, and I obviously didn't deserve it? That I felt like a failure? How could she understand any of that? What would she think of her older sister?*

Although not diagnosed, I believe I had postpartum depression or postpartum anxiety in the months following my son's birth. I reiterate that I was not diagnosed with either of these conditions. I could not have been diagnosed because I did not share what I was feeling or what I was going through with anyone—not with my husband, not with my parents, not with a friend. I kept these feelings to myself, feeling incredibly ashamed and embarrassed to even consider that having these emotions was happening to me, someone who had prayed for a child for years, someone who had done all the things to become a mother. I believe I had postpartum depression or postpartum anxiety because I have learned about these conditions in more recent years and recognize myself in their descriptions. I would also like to make it clear that having these emotions was my experience, *notwithstanding the fact that I had a great deal of help and support after I gave birth.* I was rarely "alone," there was always someone to cook a meal, hold and change the baby, and clean the house. My husband took two weeks off work, and my parents, who lived nearby, visited us almost daily. And yet, I was incredibly sad; I felt lost, I felt alone, and I felt like a fraud.

My son cried. A lot. And by "cried," I really mean *screamed.* We said he was a colicky baby because we did not know what was bothering him. At times, I was unable to console him at all. I felt inept. And deeply ashamed. I had wanted a child so badly, and now that I had one, I did not know how to be a mother. I remember breastfeeding in tears, pumping milk in tears, rocking my child to sleep in tears.

We had a beautiful bassinet beside our bed in the master bedroom. It played lullabies and vibrated or rocked, oh so gently. It was very popular and had received rave reviews. The "plan" was for James to sleep in the bassinet for the first three or so months and then transition to his crib in his room. Because I was breastfeeding, having him sleep close by in the bassinet made sense. We would be able to keep an eye on him, and it would make feedings easier.

By the time James was a month old, he was sleeping between Jeff and me in our king-sized bed. Actually, the three of us would co-sleep together for an hour, maybe two (if we were lucky) and then Jeff would spend the rest of the night in the queen bed in our guest bedroom. After a couple of weeks of this routine and our worries that James would start to roll around, Jeff moved to the guest bedroom, and I co-slept with James in our bed every night. Ultimately, co-sleeping was "the right" decision for James in that it lessened the screaming, helped him sleep throughout the night, and allowed me to rest. The decision was the right one for our child, but it did put a huge strain on our marriage. I started to feel incredibly disconnected from my husband, and I'm sure he felt the same way.

The first eight months or so following James's birth were very challenging. I had many moments of happiness, but this was not my dominant state of mind. Aside from walks in our neighborhood, we stayed home a lot. Venturing away from home or even thinking about doing it created tremendous anxiety within me. Leaving the house for more than a walk meant driving, and as soon as James was placed in his car seat (actually, within seconds of his body touching the fabric of the car seat), he would wail. So, we stayed home. I remember taking him to his routine pediatrician appointments as an infant and getting into such an anxious state that I would be sweating profusely and be physically and emotionally spent by the time we returned. I should explain that James refused to take a pacifier until about six months of age. It was grueling. Imagine a wailing infant that won't use a pacifier. It was pure torture at times. And when he discovered that he actually liked the pacifier, this same child would not stop using it until he was four years of age. Oh, the irony of it all.

Much of the first year followed this routine. It got better, eventually, but until it did, I felt like an utter failure. *Why was the gift of motherhood given to me when I clearly did not deserve it? I couldn't even console my baby! Who was I to have a child? Who was I to want to become a mother?*

Who the hell did I think I was?

I was a professional, a career woman, I handled many demanding responsibilities, people entrusted me to represent them during one of the most difficult events of their lives. But I couldn't manage parenting an infant. What the hell?!

I worried about being judged. I worried about people discovering how much of a fraud I was. I dreaded having friends visit for fear of having them witness my ineptitude, so I typically gently turned them away with excuses, which only served to isolate me further. I also didn't have the benefit of socializing virtually, as I was not yet using social media of any kind. My friends and family members had children who were a lot older, most of them in their tweens. I assumed they would not understand what I was experiencing or really have time to understand or even chat with me. I made a lot of assumptions.

But as happens, time helped. Things improved. We began to find a rhythm—our flow as a family.

When James was born, Dylan fell in love with him immediately. From what others have told me, it is not unusual for dogs to exhibit atypical destructive behavior after the birth of a child. None of that happened with Dylan. Perhaps it was in part due to *our* behavior. We tried to keep things the same as they were before the birth and to continue to be attentive parents to our dog. I was busy with the baby and therefore less attentive than I once was, but Jeff was that constant for Dylan. We continued to show our dog the love we felt for him and to treat him as a member of our family. And I believe that he felt that love.

Although it was love at first sight for Dylan, the same cannot really be said for James. He was curious about Dylan, about how his fur, ears, and tail felt when they were pulled, and all kinds of other things. He was also quick to express his disapproval and jealousy when I showed Dylan affection. We were very mindful of the fact that Dylan is a dog and that although he is an exceptionally gentle one and has never shown aggressive behavior toward dogs or people, one could never entirely predict how a dog would react to a toddler pulling his tail or trying to ride him like a horse. We ensured that there were boundaries and safeguards in place until James got a little older and could control his behavior better. It brings me so much joy and peace to see James and Dylan interact—so much so that I instinctively reach for my phone to capture these moments in a photograph. My heart is so very full when I see them together: the beautiful dog that helped change my mind and opened my heart to receive my greatest wish and blessing, my son.

Pause, reflect, lean in

- *What is a life event—for example, first-time motherhood—that in actual experience was unlike what you had envisioned?*
- *What was the internal narrative that was playing when you were in your new role as (for example) spouse, mother, newly divorced, or first-time entrepreneur?*
- *What were some ways you were able to retell the story you first told yourself?*
- *How were you able to give yourself grace and to lean into your new experience, flaws, obstacles, and all?*

Chapter Fourteen

My Motherhood Paradigm

As James's first birthday approached, I started to find the pearls of joy in motherhood. I began to focus less on what I perceived I was doing wrong, and I found pleasure in the moments of being present with my child, even the challenging ones. Returning to my law practice when my son was fifteen months old was also helpful. I felt useful, I was challenging myself in the ways that were familiar to me, and I was doing things that I believed I was good at. I was socializing more, something that I lacked for a very long time during this phase of my life.

However, my deeply held programming stood in the way of me truly harmonizing with my identity as a mother. I was raised by a stay-at-home mother, and although I got a wonderful education and pursued and followed the career I had wanted, deeply ingrained in my programming was the belief that to give the best of myself to my child, the responsibilities of a career could not compete with those of parenting.

You see, it was not that I believed I could not have a career *and* be a mother, it was that I did not believe it was possible *to do both well*: I could not be a good lawyer and a good mother at the same time. But wait a second. Isn't that belief an unfortunate foundation of our culture and society—that doing both must entail a compromise? Isn't this belief what has stopped women from historically seeking and securing careers and positions traditionally dominated by men and being paid as much as their male counterparts?

I was an educated woman who believed stoically in equality. I thought of myself as a feminist, which is one of the reasons I entered law in the first place. And yet, when it came to my own identity and my own life, my core beliefs were grounded in a paradigm that said women who have professional careers like mine could not be as *good* mothers *and* parent as effectively as those who did not. On a subconscious level, I believed that being a good mother entailed sacrificing my professional self on some level.

We are all too familiar with the mother as martyr imagery that many of us have grown up with and have been socialized to simply accept. Here's a refresher.

A good mother makes sacrifices for her family. And by "sacrifices," one means "self-sacrifice."

A good mother gives up parts of herself, her dreams and goals.

A good mother puts herself second (or third, and so on).

A good mother is selfless.

A good mother is a martyr.

Glennon Doyle speaks powerfully and eloquently about motherhood and martyrdom in her force of a book, *Untamed,* a book that I personally believe should be essential reading for the entire human race.[5] It is not easy to come up with just one meaningful passage, but here is my favorite within the beautiful pages of this book:

"Mothers have martyred themselves in their children's names since the beginning of time. We have lived as if she who disappears the most, loves the most. We have been conditioned to prove our love by slowly ceasing to exist.

What a terrible burden for children to bear—to know that they are the reason their mother stopped living. What a terrible burden for our daughters to bear—to know that if they choose to become mothers, this will be their fate, too. Because if we show them that being a martyr is the highest form of love, that is what they will become. They will feel obligated to love as well as their mothers loved, after all. They will believe they have permission to live only as fully as their mothers allowed themselves to live.

If we keep passing down the legacy of martyrdom to our daughters, with whom does it end? Which woman ever gets to live? And when does the death sentence begin? At the wedding altar? In the delivery

---

5 If you haven't read the book I urge you to do so. It will change you—in a very good way.

room? Whose delivery room—our children's or our own? When we call martyrdom love, we teach our children that when love begins, life ends. This is why Jung suggested: *There is no greater burden on a child than the unlived life of a parent.*

What if love is not the process of disappearing for the beloved but of *emerging* for the beloved? What if a mother's responsibility is teaching her children that love does not lock the lover away but *frees* her? What if a responsible mother is not one who shows her children how to slowly die but how to stay wildly alive until the day she dies? What if the call of motherhood is not to be a martyr but to be a *model*?"

I have read this section of *Untamed* several times and each time it seems to land differently for me, gifting me another layer of awareness that was not there before.

It took time, but I eventually learned to give myself grace as a mother. I learned to let go of the self-imposed expectations and the false narrative that I created about what it meant to be a mother and a parent. I became aware of the problematic and even dangerous programming that was embedded in my subconscious:

Because I wanted to become a mother for so long, because it was something that happened at the end of a complex journey, it needed to be hard.

I was unworthy if I could not rise up to this enormity of an honor and handle its challenges a certain way.

I was unworthy if I could not make motherhood mirror the picture I had of the kind of mother I wanted to be and the kind of child I wanted to have.

Read that one more time . . . how often have you thought that or even felt that way about motherhood, or perhaps it's your relationship, or that dream career? How often have you felt the unworthiness creep up simply because society dictates ideals a certain way? How long have you hung yourself dry, depleted, burnt out, and spent on the noose of self-sacrifice and martyrdom?

I gave myself love and compassion and I trusted that everything I needed to know, everything I needed to have to parent my son was already there, within me. I stopped searching for answers in books and on the internet, I stopped comparing myself to others, including my own mother who was for me the epitome of a "good mother" and who I believed I had to emulate in my parenting.

Glennon Doyle talks about the "Knowing," something that deeply resonated with me when I read *Untamed*:

"Eventually I sank deep enough to find a new level inside me that I'd never known existed. This place is underneath: low, deep, quiet, still. There are no voices there, not even my own. All I can hear down there is my breath."

"I can *know* things down at this level that I can't on the chaotic surface. Down here, when I pose a question about my life—in words or abstract images—I sense a nudge. The nudge guides me toward the next precise thing, and then, when I silently acknowledge the nudge—it fills me. The Knowing feels like warm liquid gold filling my veins and solidifying just enough to make me feel steady, certain."

I started to listen to *my knowing* when my son was a year old. I began to "sink beneath the swirling surf of words, fear, expectations, conditioning, and advice—and feel for the Knowing."

Before I knew it, my son grew into a little boy. And I grew too, stronger and more confident, more *knowing* of myself as a mother. The twos weren't so terrible—they were actually pretty good. The threes, fours, and fives were in many ways a delight. I enjoy parenting more and more each year. My son is now six, and I am astounded by the little boy he has grown into and by how he enriches my life each day.

My son is a very affectionate and empathetic child. The other day when he was hugging and kissing me, I said, "I'd better enjoy this while I can. One day you'll no longer want to hug and kiss me and say you're too old for my cuddles." He looked directly at me, hugged me tighter and said the words that I will never forget for as long as I live: "What are you talking about, Mama? I will always want to hug and kiss you, Mama. I will never stop."

When I tell him "I love you sooooo much," he smiles, pulls me into a tight hug (his hugs are full body experiences), and says, "I love you even more! I love you the most!" James often tells me, "I have the best mom." He writes out the phrase when he journals for school and in the birthday and Mother's Day cards he makes. I was raised by the best mother in the world and now my son tells me I am the best mom. What a gift!

Do I need this validation of my parenting or the strength of the bond I know I have with my son? No. Does it make me feel good? Yes. Does it instill confidence about my parenting? Yes. Does it make me grateful for every difficult, taxing, painful moment, every single moment before then and for any challenge to come? Yes, very much.

Those experiences did more than make me beam with joy and pride. They shook me to my core. They rattled the negative self-talk that had been playing in my head, whispering that I haven't achieved the goals I set out to achieve months before. Those experiences reminded me of my "why." They reminded me of the gift that I had been given. They broke open my heart and allowed the gratitude to pour inside and shine its beautiful warm light.

I am a mother to a delightful, empathetic, intelligent, funny, witty, loving boy.

I am the luckiest woman in the world.

Although I felt alone during my fertility and motherhood journey, I really wasn't. There was always "a Higher Power, a higher intelligence and plan at work," as author Lalah Delia explains in *Vibrate Higher Daily*. I didn't know it then, but there was another force working behind the scenes. While I was forcing *when* and *how* I would become a mother, the Universe had other ideas. She was treading lightly, but powerfully. I was striving for motherhood from a low vibration, a place of scarcity and urgency. I eventually harmonized with the vibration of the Universe and what her higher plan was for me.

Similarly, when I was a new mother, I was not harmonizing with the vibration of the mother I wanted to be—a mother who was at peace with herself and her child, a mother who trusted in her intuition, a mother who loved herself and was kind to herself. Instead of looking at my child and being grateful for what I had, I kept asking myself why I didn't have "an easier baby," one who slept in his crib, one who didn't cry so much, one who was easier to console. I was thinking and behaving from that familiar place of lack.

I finally started to see what I did have. I began to see that I had exactly the son who was meant to be my son. Our beautiful boy has his mother's eyes. But he also has his mother's tenacity, sensitivity, empathy, ear for and love of music, and love of animals. Our beautiful boy has his father's nose and cheekbones. But he also has his father's curiosity, imagination, love of words and reading, and love of nature.

During this unprecedented time, navigating the challenges of daily life during a pandemic, I have been present like never before. Ironically, I think I have been more present than I was when my child was an infant, even during the fifteen months of maternity leave. Although I devoted myself to caring for my new baby at that time, a large part of me was tied up in a mindset of survival. I now parent from a mindset of abundance, and instead of merely surviving, I truly believe I am thriving, and consequently, so is my son, in infinite ways. I have seen my child grow physically and emotionally. Witnessing this beautiful growth and understanding that I had something to do with it is incredibly gratifying and a joyous blessing.

Pause, reflect, lean in

- *On a blank sheet of paper or in your journal, list all the desires, things, or opportunities you've received (with ease or after years of waiting and longing).*

- *Now, go through every single desire, thing, or opportunity you've received and beside each of them, write down the first feeling that surfaced when you first received these.*

- *Notice if these were feelings of abundance, gratitude, confidence, or lack, unworthiness, insecurity, or perhaps even guilt.*

- *On a new page, write a list of all the things that make you who you are. For instance, "I am smart, intelligent, and goal oriented . . ." and then add "AND I can be flexible and stay open to new perspectives." OR "I can be a devoted wife, mother, daughter, AND still love my career." Complement each inherent strength you have with "AND I can . . ."*

- *Read this letter aloud every time you feel those doubts, inadequacies, or lack surface. Welcome to rewiring the motherhood paradigm. The journey starts with us, and the cycles end with us choosing to shift them.*

Chapter Fifteen

The Mystery of the Mind

The mind is a powerful thing. At the risk of oversimplifying, what you think *is* what you get. Or, more accurately, *how you think* plays a huge part in the results you get. What I'm referring to goes beyond "positive thinking." It is about thinking a particular way.

The mind is also highly misunderstood.

I used to think of the mind as the brain. While the brain is a physical part of the body, the mind is something quite different. Though the brain is one distinct element of the body, the mind exists throughout the body. Let me explain.

The mind is made up of two parts: the conscious mind and the subconscious mind. There are various ways to label these parts, "conscious and subconscious," "conscious and unconscious," and so on. I will use the labels "conscious" and "subconscious" here.

The conscious mind is what people typically think of when they consider the mind; it is the thinking mind or the educated mind. The conscious mind is like a sponge in that it receives information from the outside world through the five senses: sight, hearing, scent, taste, and touch. The conscious mind is shaped by what is witnessed and by what the environment does.

The subconscious mind is the emotional mind. The early Greeks referred to the subconscious mind as the heart. When we impress the picture of what we desire on our subconscious mind, meaning that if we really want and desire that thing, and we internalize the image of that thing, the image moves into form with and through us. The subconscious mind is not limited by the five senses. The subconscious mind is guided by the six higher faculties. They are reason, memory, perception, imagination, intuition, and will. These help us achieve success and what we desire in life.

Our conscious mind has the ability to limit and discard the information it collects. Assessment, judgment, and criticism originates here. If, however, we become emotionally involved with an idea, we move it from our conscious to our subconscious mind. And that, my friends, is where something magical happens. The subconscious mind expresses that which is impressed upon it. At the risk of oversimplifying, that is how thinking transforms to action, and finally, to results.

We are preprogrammed at birth (or more accurately, at conception) with a particular set of information, a program, if you will, that structures our thinking and guides us to behave a certain way. This information is called a paradigm. Although we may come into the world with paradigms, they are not absolute—paradigms can change, and we can acquire new paradigms throughout our lifetime. It is a beautiful thing.

You can think of logic as driving a person's behavior at a conscious level and a paradigm as powering a person's behavior at a subconscious level. The mental pull you feel to choose one thought or idea over another is your paradigm. And because thoughts and ideas lead to action, it is the paradigm that is at the root of behavior. Thus, the subconscious mind, not the conscious mind, directs action and ultimately determines results.

We have relationship paradigms, money paradigms, food paradigms, parenting paradigms, career paradigms—all kinds of paradigms. Perhaps your upbringing was rooted in the paradigm that wealth promotes greed and that people with money are selfish or immoral. Perhaps you developed the paradigm that relationships are hard and that love is ephemeral and tenuous as a result of your parents' divorce or your own divorce.

Understanding the subconscious mind is critical to understanding the power of paradigms. The subconscious mind is vital to actualizing our wants and desires. If one has programming that says wealthy people are evil, then that person will not likely acquire wealth no matter how educated they are or how hard they work.

Challenging and questioning a paradigm creates discomfort, and most people are averse to discomfort. They therefore prefer to remain in the comfort of their paradigm, even if doing so is generating results that they do not desire. Constant spaced repetition is required to change a paradigm. Through this repetition, habits are formed. Changing and transforming a paradigm changes one's mindset. And our mindset is the lens through which we process circumstances and the world around us and the framework through which we think, feel, and act. It is the conduit to our results, and it is extremely powerful.

Stanford psychologist Carol Dweck's research on mindset is instructive and illuminating. A fixed mindset assumes that our abilities cannot be meaningfully changed; they are static in the sense that what we come into this life with is what we have and we either have a skill, trait, and ability, or we do not. A fixed mindset says that our intelligence, creative ability, and personality are immutably ingrained traits. A growth mindset, on the other hand, assumes that our characteristics and abilities can evolve. It welcomes challenge; indeed, it *thrives* on challenge and sees "failure" as an opportunity and springboard for growth.

I am also familiar with mindset as a continuum or spectrum. Survival mindset is at one end, maintaining mindset and managing mindset are mid-spectrum, and thriving mindset is at the other end.[6] The survival and maintaining mindsets can be considered "fixed"

6The mindset spectrum I summarize was referred to by Dr. Wayne Hammond, Founding Partner and Chief Science Officer at Flourishing Life Technologies, Presenting at Certified Coaches Federation (CCF) Emerge Summit August 2020.

mindsets and the managing and thriving mindsets can be considered "growth" mindsets.

Someone with a survival mindset is disengaged and unmotivated; they approach life as "all or nothing," "perfection," or "failure." There is no room for progress or growth in this outlook.

Someone with a maintaining mindset is risk averse and lacks trust. They are protective in their outlook. They remain fully within their comfort zone and are extremely apprehensive about venturing outside of it.

Someone with a managing mindset has a cautious outlook, is productive, but fears failure. They are reluctant to step away from the familiar, and when they do, it is quite rare.

And finally, someone with a thriving mindset is forward-thinking, optimistic, unafraid to *leap* out of their comfort zone, and *prepared* to fail because they have the awareness that this, too, is growth.

There is some fluidity along this spectrum because people can move along it, in either direction, through life. For example, someone may fall into the category of having a growth mindset and may view themselves this way, but once they experience an event such as the end of a marriage, they may exhibit more of a survival mindset.

While working as a resilience coach, it was not unusual to see a client move forward and back along this spectrum depending upon what they were experiencing at a particular point in time and how they had progressed with our work, particularly in the initial stages of the coaching process. The goal, obviously, was to help my client cultivate the ability to remain in more of a growth mindset and to approach a thriving mindset, whatever events and challenges life brought their way.

It is common for those navigating separation and divorce to struggle with their mindset. It is easy to view their circumstances from a place of lack and to focus on the changes they are experiencing—from living as a couple to losing their romantic partner or spouse of many years, having to move out of the home where they, their partner, and their children resided for years, having to make unanticipated and often uncomfortable financial decisions, and having to manage shifting relationships with friends and relatives. It is easy to view and process these changes as ones of loss and not nearly as easy to see them as opportunities for growth, evolution, and new beginnings. Learning to cultivate an awareness that you are the creator of your life post-separation or divorce may be challenging, but it is absolutely critical to effectively navigating the legal issues and profound changes in this life transition. And getting the help of not only a competent, compassionate, and experienced family lawyer but also another professional such as a resilience coach is necessary to emerge from this experience thriving rather than merely surviving.

Pause, reflect, lean in

- *Do you believe you have a growth mindset or a fixed mindset?*
- *Where do you see yourself along the mindset continuum?*

- *When faced with challenges, do you tend to lean into them or lean out of them?*
- *What would it feel like to merely survive? To maintain? To manage and thrive?*
- *What are the thoughts/words you grew up hearing about in terms of money, marriage, love, career, parenthood? What kinds of actions did you witness?*
- *Remember, what we hear and witness shapes our consciousness and subconscious. Be it positive or negative, we still hold the power to reshape and rewire our subconscious thoughts.*

Chapter Sixteen

THE FERTILITY MINDSET AND THE NARRATIVE OF MISCARRIAGE

When I began my fertility journey, I was thinking and behaving from a scarcity mindset. No question. I did not know it then, but I certainly understand it now. I was focused on what I did not have, which then led to all-consuming resentment and feelings of despair. It also led to actions that were extensions of those feelings. I took action—monitored my ovulation cycle, sought out the opinions of doctors, underwent tests and surgeries, and went through fertility treatments—with urgency and struggle.

There was a time that I believed my career/ambition was the cause of my infertility. I chose and lived a stressful job. I chose to work eleven-hour days. I chose to take work home with me or go to the office on weekends. I made my choices, prioritized my career, and was rewarded with infertility. In constructing this narrative, I was painting myself as a victim of the "selfish" choices I had made. I was creating victimization out of my circumstances.

It seems almost silly to articulate it now, but those were my thoughts. I was basically looking for something to blame my infertility on and the "something" that I decided on was me. *I* brought infertility upon myself. *I* made my choice—career over motherhood— and I was now aptly rewarded.

> *What did you expect? You waited too long.*
> *You made your choice. You chose career success and money.*
> *Oh, so now you think you're ready to be a mother. Well,*
> *you're a little late to the game.*

This is the story I told myself.

I started my career during a time when women were breaking all kinds of barriers. Just over one half of my law school graduating class was female. That was 1999. This percentage was likely unheard of twenty or even ten years before then. However, for all the wonderful progress women had made, obtaining a professional degree, then pursuing a career in that field and seeing it through, was a completely different story. I am likely generalizing to a certain extent, but my comments are simply based on what I saw happening around me. When I began practicing and throughout much of my career, I felt as if the predominant culture was one where women were expected to *choose between* motherhood or a career as a lawyer. One or the other. Not both. However, if you did manage to do both, you were considered less of a lawyer in some ways because you could not give *the law* your full and complete attention, 100 percent of you. If you were a successful lawyer and you had children, then it was assumed that you not only had help with childcare but you also had a live-in caregiver or at least full-time daycare for your child, extended after-school care, etc. The dominant view, from my perspective anyway, was that it was not possible to have children and excel at the profession of law or, at any rate, to excel the way men were excelling.

I was far from vocal about my experience with recurrent pregnancy loss. Before writing this book, I did not really talk about my two miscarriages. People very close to me knew about them, but I didn't truly talk about what I experienced. Perhaps I was discouraged to share my pain by the all-too-prevalent narrative that miscarriage and recurrent pregnancy loss are "common experiences." Perhaps I was reluctant to say much because my miscarriages were "early." Reminding myself of how short my pregnancies were, how early the losses occurred, were the themes of the narratives I was familiar with and that I recited to myself. I essentially talked myself into believing that the losses I had were "better," "lesser," and "easier" since I had not been pregnant "for long," and since I had not been *noticeably* pregnant to the outside world. I talked myself into minimizing my pain, sorrow, and loss.

There is nothing common about the experience of losing a pregnancy. It is a deeply personal and subjective event. No two experiences of pregnancy loss can possibly be alike. Although my miscarriages occurred at approximately the same gestation (about eight weeks), the events and how I lived through and after each of them were quite different.

My first miscarriage was a crushing shock. It was the first time I felt the emotional and physical pain of losing a pregnancy. Physically, it was an ordeal that seemed never-ending. Emotionally, it was, until then, the most devastating experience of my life. It broke me down in ways I could not have imagined or for which I could have prepared. Becoming pregnant through IVF was my first pregnancy. Although the actual pregnancy itself was a few weeks long, the journey to get there, including the actual IVF process itself, felt incredibly long. Having my pregnancy taken away from me a few short weeks after learning of it felt like my insides were ripped out of me.

My second miscarriage occurred after natural conception. It took place slightly earlier than the first pregnancy loss. Physically, it began exceptionally painfully, with an intensity that I was not prepared for, but the event was not as prolonged. Emotionally, the experiences differed greatly. It was my first natural pregnancy, and it was a complete surprise. And this gift was snatched away before I even had the chance to celebrate it and share it with others.

Society seems to assess the severity of miscarriage depending upon how early or late in the pregnancy the loss occurred. I did the same myself before experiencing pregnancy loss, and I did it when I had my own miscarriage. There appears to be a common assumption that miscarriage is worse when it occurs later, but later than when? Is a woman who miscarried at seven or eight weeks somehow absolved of pain and the feelings that she has lost her baby? Are the tears that woman shed fewer? Is the heartache subdued? Is her grief less worthy of comfort, compassion, and empathy because her loss occurred "early?"

When we generalize the experience of miscarriage, we dismiss the enormity of the experience and the profound and lasting effect it has on a woman physically, emotionally, mentally, and spiritually. To generalize in this manner is nothing short of insulting to the women who have lived this profound loss that they never truly "get over." And when we label a miscarriage as "early," with all its attendant connotations of "easier," "less painful," "*better*," what are we saying to the woman who is mourning?

Looking back, I now understand that I downplayed what had happened to me. I feared the judgment of those around me. I was ashamed that I had made the difficult decision to pursue assisted reproduction, had invested so much of myself in the IVF process, restructured my professional life to do so, and had ultimately failed. I judged myself harshly. Was there any evidence that others considered me a failure? Absolutely not. In fact, I received an outpouring of support from family, friends, and colleagues. Although some did not really know how to express their feelings, I understood what they were trying to convey, and I appreciated it. And there was nothing judgmental in their behavior toward me. It was self-judgment.

Writing this part of the book immediately takes me back to my two miscarriages as if they were yesterday, notwithstanding that they occurred nearly eleven and seven years ago. I may have healed, but I have never "gotten over it." How can I? I experienced the loss of a pregnancy twice. And while the loss occurred earlier in the pregnancy than some, this timing did not lessen my mourning. I moved forward after each of my miscarriages, but I never forgot them. I don't believe I ever will. *They were mine. They were a part of me.* It may have been only for a matter of weeks, but they were a part of me and lived inside of me. And I will forever remember those lives that never made it here earthside. And that is okay.

Although my pregnancy losses will forever be a part of my experience, that does not mean that I have not been able to heal. Healing does not mean forgetting your wounds or ignoring them. Healing entails acknowledgment and acceptance of your wounds but also resilience and growth in moving forward and rising from them. This process is not linear, but growth rarely is.

Pause, reflect, lean in

- *When you experienced loss (no matter what it is), how did you feel? What are the emotions that surfaced during and after? Did you share it with anyone around you? How was it received? Was there space held for you?*
- *Looking back, do you still feel these emotions? Do you share these with a trusted confidant?*
- *How did this loss help you grow, become resilient, and evolve?*
- *What is one thing you would say to your prior self?*

Chapter Seventeen

How to Raise Your Vibrational Frequency and Live at Cause

For many years of my life, I was reactionary in how I thought about and responded to events around me and to my circumstances. It was easy to point the finger at a situation, person, or event to explain and justify what was happening *to* me, or not happening *for* me.

Learning to think and act from the inside, rather than the outside, was a new phenomenon. Questioning a long-held paradigm and then replacing that paradigm with a new pattern of thinking, feeling, and behaving was a process—and still is. I owe a lot of this process to my coaching training and certification, as well as my experience working as a coach and helping people through various life transitions. I also owe it to having had the opportunity to work with my own coach. Yes, even coaches benefit from and need coaches.

Cultivating and subsequently applying new paradigms is a process. It takes time, effort, commitment, and accountability. It is most certainly a long game. Having said that, there are things that you can do in your everyday life to take control of your thinking, to shape your thinking, and to conduct your life living intentionally and living on purpose from the inside out rather than being the object of outside forces.

Vibration, energy, frequency, the law of attraction. These terms and concepts used to sound like a whole lotta fluff to me. That was then. Now, they evoke something different.

The law of attraction states that what you send out into the Universe is what you will attract back to you. To put it simply, all thoughts eventually turn into things. When you live your life from a place of scarcity, you attract more scarcity into your life. When you bemoan your circumstances and focus on what is lacking in love, in a partner, in a job, you stoke those flames—you invite more lack into your relationships and possibly even repel potential relationships or job and career opportunities.

Our vibration is responsible for everything we experience in our lives—our thoughts, feelings, actions, and finally, our results. We emit a vibration, a frequency, or an energy into the world, and it attracts more of itself back to us. If we vibrate with love, abundance, and gratitude, we will attract that energy back into ourselves and our lives. Our energetic vibration is our constant companion. It drives our thoughts, feelings, and actions and ultimately, our results.

There are things that you can do as part of your daily life to raise your vibrational frequency. I have found the following helpful in raising my vibration so that I am at cause and co-creating my life. Consider these tips to incorporate as you see fit. If you're doubtful about their effectiveness, then I gently encourage you to try them out for seven, fourteen, or ideally twenty-one days and observe what happens. You really don't have anything to lose, but you have much to gain.

PRACTICING GRATITUDE DAILY

The popularity of cultivating a gratitude practice is growing. Gratitude lists have become all the rage. When I use the phrase "practicing gratitude daily," I am not referring to making a gratitude list and leaving it at that. I'm referring to intentionally infusing your thoughts, feelings, and actions with gratitude and appreciation for the elements of the life that you have (your child, your partner, your parents, your friends, your job, your home, your community, your health, your creative skills, your talents, etc.). It is about expressing wholehearted gratitude for what you have rather than bemoaning what you believe you lack.

Why practice gratitude? What is all the fuss about?

Gratitude means being thankful or appreciative for that which we have. Gratitude opens our hearts and souls, our consciousness, to receiving. When we are open, we are essentially preparing ourselves to receive more. By receiving, I am not referring to greed or gluttony or the belief that we are entitled to have something at the expense of someone else. Receiving, in my opinion, is allowing yourself to embrace all the opportunities around you. It's about feeling you are worthy of things coming your way and permitting yourself to accept them instead of pushing them away. Much of what we believe we are unable to achieve has been shut out by us. We reject it. We are so closed off by struggle, resentment, and anger that we do not even see that the very thing we want is just ahead of us, ready to enter our lives with ease. Many of us often have the exact recipe in front of us and are asked to whip something spectacular out of the ingredients that are already present in our life, which in this case is our circumstances. We are simply missing one key ingredient—a shift in our perspective.

A great way to begin a gratitude practice and to have some fun with it at the same time is to initiate a thirty-day challenge. Post an invitation to the challenge on social media and make it an interactive experience. Make it a family interactive experience by spending a few minutes each day (perhaps at the dinner table) sharing one thing for which each family member is grateful. These are surefire ways to raise your vibration and, in the process, raise the vibration of others!

CREATING AN IDEAL SELF-IMAGE

Our self-image is extraordinarily powerful. It has a profound effect on how we live our lives.

Who do you want to be? When I ask this question, I am not only referring to the job or career that you desire. I am referring to the kind of person that you want to be.

How do you want to feel about yourself and what you do?

Get imaginative and become emotionally involved in this exercise. Create that self-image in as much detail as possible. Do you want to be a successful entrepreneur with a thriving business, consistent clients, a waitlist of people who want to work with you, exciting projects, and collaboration opportunities? Do you envision yourself as a thought leader in your particular industry, with a large audience, robust client base, a regular media presence, and speaking engagements? Do you desire a close and loving relationship of fluid communication and intimate experiences with your spouse?

Our self-image is the foundation for what we do in every element of our lives. It sets the tone for what we achieve and the life we create.

Begin a habit of journaling your ideal self-image in the morning. You'll be surprised how this affects your mindset and how you go about your day.

WRITING AND RECITING A LIFE SCRIPT

Have you ever written a story about the life you desire? Writing out your ideal life script daily is very powerful. It can be incorporated with writing out your self-image during your daily journaling practice.

What are your goals?

What do you desire?

What do you really want?

Writing out your life script, in the present tense, as if it is happening at this moment in time, will help solidify the vision of what you wish to achieve and the goals you want to attain. The repetition of this exercise reinforces the thoughts and feelings that will propel you to intentional action.

Reciting the script you have written is a way to solidify the practice. Saying the words out loud to yourself impresses them upon your subconscious mind. I know several people who recite their life script aloud in front of a mirror, as it helps them be more present in the activity and more intentional in the exercise.

It is one thing to write out a sentence or two, it is quite another to repeatedly read that sentence aloud so that your ears hear it. You inevitably process your story differently by observing the words on a page as you write them down and then hearing yourself recite them.

Be the author of your life script! You're in charge—you are the writer of your story.

LEAVING PEOPLE WITH THE IMPRESSION OF INCREASE

I like to think of this exercise as the companion to practicing gratitude. Both prepare us to receive.

Leaving others with the impression of increase means going about your day with the specific intention of leaving others better than you found them.

How often do we even think about how our seemingly mundane or carefree actions are affecting those around us? How often do we turn our minds to how our exchange with the cab driver or coffee barista has made them feel?

Moving intentionally through your day with the goal of leaving others better than you found them—making a positive difference in their lives, even for a short moment—is quite remarkable. And yet, so easy.

However, do not confuse this exercise with trading or being transactional in our interactions. When we trade, we expect something in return for our act of generosity or kindness. When we leave someone with the impression of increase, we are not expecting reciprocation.

Show kindness, care, empathy, and appreciation each time you interact with the cashier, cab driver, cleaning staff, coffee barista, mail carrier, neighbor, child's teacher, bank teller, your employer, your employee, your contractor, your spouse, your child, your parent, your friend . . . and the list goes on. Witnessing the effects of this behavior—the smile on the barista's face, the nod of thanks from your neighbor, the note of thanks from your friend, the growing confidence of your child—uplifts you, raises your energy, and prepares you to receive more.

FOLLOWING YOUR INTUITION AND CULTIVATING YOUR CREATIVITY

Adults typically act from a place of logic. We think things through, make a decision, and proceed.

What if you try something different? Take a particular action, and not because it will lead to something or is a step to something else.

Do it because it makes you *feel good*. Do it simply because *you want to*, because you *desire to*.

Think about the last time you watched children engaged in play and social interaction. Did you pay close attention to what was going on? Witnessing playful energy in action is quite something.

While logic drives much of adult behavior, intuition and emotion drive children's behavior. Children choose an activity, a toy, or a game because of the way it makes them feel. If they've previously done the activity or played with the particular toy, they remember how they felt and they choose to repeat and duplicate the experience. If it is the first time they are doing something, they play with the toy or engage in the activity because they are drawn to it for some reason. They are curious. They follow their intuition, and it leads them to play with the toy or to choose the action.

Children don't rationalize whether they should do x, y, or z. They don't make a pros and cons list. They act on instinct and intuition. If they are drawn to something, they do it.

Take an afternoon (even better, take a few days) and consistently engage in activities that light you up. Do them because they make you feel good. Don't consider any other motivation, and don't overthink it. Listen to your intuition and follow it. If you're called to take a nap, do it. If you're called to go for a walk on the beach, do it. If you're called to get out your brushes, canvas, and paints, create that piece of art.

When you're done, take note of how you feel; really pay attention. And while you're still in this energy, on this high vibration, turn your mind to your regular responsibilities or a list of tasks that need to be completed. Perhaps it is something that you've put off for some time or are procrastinating about beginning. I bet that those tasks and responsibilities will be completed with more ease and flow than would have been the case had you not engaged in the intuitive actions that preceded them. Try it.

Doing this exercise regularly and for a prolonged period of time will create a beautiful shift. Your energy levels will increase, and you will move to a frequency where you will reignite your self-confidence and find your spirit.

When I am cultivating my writing, giving time and space to my craft, and leaning into my passion and joy, I notice it's impact in my personal and professional relationships and in how I deal with my responsibilities. Cultivating your creativity and pursuing actions or interests that make you feel good raises your vibration and has lasting effects in other areas. Creativity creates ripples elsewhere. And isn't that what we desire more of anyway? A life full of creativity, feel-good vibrations, joy, and intentional living.

FORGIVING OTHERS AND FORGIVING YOURSELF

We raise our vibrational frequency with forgiveness.

Forgive those who you never imagined you would be able to forgive. It could be a former spouse who was unfaithful. It could be a friend with whom you parted ways after a serious disagreement. It could be a neighbor with whom you had a row. It could be a relative you have not spoken to in years.

A common misconception abounds as far as forgiveness is concerned. We view forgiving as giving up something of ourselves—our dignity, our "rights"—and somehow compromising ourselves in the process. But that is not the case at all. When you forgive, both yourself and the other person, you are cultivating self-love. The act of forgiveness may have benefits for the person being forgiven, but I believe that the true beneficiary of the act is the person doing the forgiving.

At first, it can be extraordinarily challenging and uncomfortable to forgive, but the challenge and discomfort are nothing compared to the beauty of how freeing the act of forgiveness is. To forgive is to release pain, anger, resentment—the things that hinder you from living your best life.

Forgiveness is a blessing.

Raising your energetic vibration and living intentionally doesn't require you to pack your bags and jet off to Bali or Big Sur. It requires you to infuse intentionality in every part of your life, starting with your thoughts, your words, and your actions. It requires you to refine yourself, moment after moment, challenge after challenge. It requires you to seek growth. It requires you to celebrate your life and who you are, to own who you are, flaws and all, and to love yourself, even when everything around you is falling apart. It requires you to believe in your ability to be the co-creator of your life. It requires you to trust in possibilities when all around you there only exist limitations. It requires you to transcend your logic and lean into faith, trust, intuition.

It requires you to trust your ability to attract your desires, live your best life, and do what it takes, with alignment, to get there.

Pause, reflect, lean in

- *What are three things for which you are grateful? Go deep. Feel into the emotion.*

- *What are your goals?*

- *What do you desire?*

- *What do you really want?*

- *When was the last time you allowed yourself to play, love, laugh, live freely? When was the last time you were immersed in an activity for pure pleasure and enjoyment?*

- *Is there someone you need to forgive and release? Have you shared that with them?*

- *If this person is no longer a part of your life and communication isn't possible, write a letter to them and read it out loud to yourself. Look in the mirror as you do so. Feel into the energy and emotion behind your words and send those vibrations to this individual. You've just channeled energy toward them and released the energetic cords that kept you tethered together.*

- *Notice how you feel in your body as you move through these journal questions daily. Notice the pain shifting and releasing, the frequency rising, and your perspective expanding along with your life and its possibilities.*

Chapter Eighteen

Nothing Says Gratitude Like a Cancer Diagnosis

In September 2020, I had a needle biopsy under mammogram of my right breast (also known as a stereotactic biopsy). It was not my first breast biopsy, as I had several between 2010 and 2014. However, it was my first biopsy since becoming a mother.

A few days after the procedure, I was sitting in my doctor's office being told that I had ductal carcinoma in situ (DCIS), or cancerous cells in the ducts of my breast. I had sat across from my doctor many times before then and had been given very different results. You see, I have dense or fibrous breasts, meaning that I have firmer tissue, nodules, and lumps, which is my "normal."

I was told I needed surgery. I was not in the least prepared for the words I was hearing. I was stunned. And I was scared.

I recall my doctor used the words "lumpectomy" and "partial mastectomy" interchangeably. The power that terminology wields is quite remarkable. Hearing the word "mastectomy" terrified me. It was also difficult to reconcile the term with the way my doctor was describing my cancer as being "precancer" or "early stage." I tried not to think too much about the word and concentrated on the fact that the cells were discovered when and where they were. Although I did not entirely understand it at that moment, I was being given good news.

I had surgery three weeks after my diagnosis. I have had surgery before, but the experience of waiting at a hospital to be taken into surgery, alone, during a pandemic, is very different. I was highly emotional. I remember sitting in the surgical waiting room, attached to my IV, my tears soaking my mask, and my hands shaking.

The procedure went well, and the area that was removed was not very large. I had a lot of discomfort, swelling, and pain following the surgery, which was expected.

I was healing well physically and was ready for my oncology consultation, followed by a consultation with a radiology oncologist. I liked the radiology oncologist immediately. He explained that given the size of the cancerous area and all the other circumstances, my prognosis was good. I underwent just over three weeks of daily radiation treatment in December, my final treatment occurring two days before Christmas. The process was inconvenient, and the procedure caused pain, swelling, and fatigue. But it could have been a lot worse.

My pain and discomfort worsened in the months following the radiation treatment. I was warned it may happen. I still continue to experience discomfort, the pigmentation of my right breast remains somewhat darker (resembling a tan), and my right breast is fuller and feels heavier than the left. Wearing any kind of bra for more than a couple of hours is also a challenge, but I view these as minor inconveniences and irritations.

I have been monitored annually since 2010. Annual (and occasionally six-month) bilateral ultrasounds and mammograms have been a part of my life since then. I used to complain a lot. It wasn't easy to rush from a hospital in the east end to my midtown law practice, holding ice packs against my chest while I drafted urgent court material or convened a phone meeting. It wasn't easy to keep track of the tests and biopsies (was it the left or right breast the last time?). But I did it.

For almost three of those years, I was having these procedures between IVF cycles. It sounds unreal to me now, but it's true. I distinctly remember the first of these biopsies and the conversation I had with the young nurse who was preparing me for the procedure. We chatted about our lives, and she asked me if I had children. I told her "not yet," and that I was about to undergo my first IVF cycle. She was very happy for me, told me that I would make a wonderful mother, and wished me well on my fertility journey. I was extremely touched by her kind words and that is probably why I remember them nearly eleven years later.

When I was in the midst of this cancer journey, my emotions ran wild. I was sad, incredibly worried, and angry. Mostly, I felt resentful because of the timing of my diagnosis: "Why didn't this happen before I became a mother?" "Why did this happen when I have a young child?"

But I was a mother. I had a young child. And with every element of my being, I was going to move forward, follow the advice of my doctors, and get the treatment that I needed to manage my diagnosis. I would do everything I could, and I would do so with gratitude, love, and peace. I had learned these lessons well from my journey through infertility, and I knew that I could apply them in this context as well. And that is exactly what I did.

I now live my life being proactive about my health and being more conscious about what I eat and drink. It isn't easy, and I often stray from the path that is best for me, but I keep trying and I keep going. Because I had DCIS, I now have mammograms, ultrasounds, and MRI imaging every six months. Six or seven years ago, I would have viewed it all as a huge nuisance. I now view it as a blessing. It is my new normal, and I'll gladly take it.

Life-changing moments aren't solely relegated to health diagnoses alone. No, life-changing moments can occur within a split second. The loss of a loved one. The end of a relationship or friendship. The loss of a career you spent decades building. Each of these moments hit us differently. What matters is the power we hold over ourselves when faced with these moments. It doesn't mean that heartache isn't involved, or that tears won't be shed. It doesn't mean every single day will be sunshine and rainbows. Nor does it mean that every waking moment will be spent being resentful, angry, or grieving. Within every single gut-wrenching moment there is a silver lining to be found, a lesson to be learned, and a blessing to be uncovered.

Pause, reflect, lean in

- What are some life-changing moments you can recall?

- Perhaps you have experienced the end of a relationship or marriage?

- Perhaps you have grieved the loss of a family member?

- Have you said good-bye to a pet?

- Have you navigated a serious illness?

- Perhaps you have lost your employment or had to close down your business?

- Can you uncover the gifts within your life-changing moments?

Chapter Nineteen

And Sometimes Your Gratitude Will Be Tested

The real test of cultivating a gratitude practice lies in how you navigate the life-changing moments we have discussed throughout this book. It is one thing to navigate a serious illness yourself, but it's a whole new thing when you are dealing with an illness or terminal illness of someone close to you. Over this past year, just as I thought we were turning a new corner after navigating my own challenges, my mother's health took a turn for the worse.

Seeing my beautiful, strong, and formidable force of a mother decline over the last two years of her life was unlike anything I have experienced. And then seeing her dramatically decline in a matter of three days after being admitted to hospital was the most painful thing

I have witnessed in my lifetime. My heart broke apart into a million fragments when I was finally allowed to visit her. How was it that less than a week before she was cooking some soup for my son? Seeing your beloved parent in their final days is traumatic. It struck me to my core and will forever be imprinted in my soul.

My mother was the most alive, vivacious, and vibrant person I knew. She has been and always will be, to me, the personification of integrity, strength, resilience, and love. My mother is the one who gave me life, the one who gave me strength when I thought myself weak, the one who reminded me of my abilities and talents, the one who always told me I "can be whoever and whatever I want," the one who held me up when I was falling down, and the one who calmed, soothed, and healed me for nearly forty-eight years. My mother gave me so much love and that love was limitless, unconditional, and enduring.

With her passing early this year, I felt a hole in the depths of my soul like no other. I honestly did not know I could cry that much. Although I know death is an inevitable passage of being human, I never imagined I could feel such sorrow, such heart-wrenching pain.

Then I became angry—angrier than I have ever been. *Now? After all that she has endured for years living with pain interrupted by discomfort and brief moments of respite? Now? Months after the birth of her fourth grandchild, my beautiful niece?*

I was angry at God.

I was angry at the doctors and nurses.

I was angry at everyone and everything.

I was angry at this cruel, awful, terrible thing that was allowed to happen.

I stayed in this place for longer than I had wanted. But I had to. I had to sit with my feelings, even if they were ugly.

And then I began to slowly shift.

As I lived with my sadness and grief, I shifted. I realized something. God was being anything but cruel, awful, and terrible.

My mother had lived for several years with more than one serious illness. I left the firm where I worked when I did because her health had continued to decline, and I wanted to be there for her as much as I could. And then she was with us for a further nineteen months. For that I am eternally grateful.

I feel immense gratitude that my mother was there for my son's birth and that she watched him grow for the first five-and-a-half years of his life. I am grateful that she was able to hold her fourth grandchild, my delightful niece who will be eleven months old when this book is published. I am grateful that this amazing, wonderful, generous woman gave me strength and love through my cancer diagnosis, surgery, and radiation treatment in the few months before her passing.

I was able to visit with my mother the day before she passed away. I told her I loved her and held her hand. I quietly sang the song "You

Are My Sunshine" while choking back tears and then relenting to their flow. Although she could not speak to me, I saw the flash of recognition in her eyes. Of course, she recognized the lyrics. She had sung them countless times to me, my siblings, and more recently, to her grandson. She also heard them sung to her by my son, her face beaming with pride and love. And now, these were the last words I would sing to her.

Before my mother passed away, my pregnancy losses were the most difficult events I experienced. Those were incredible losses that forever changed me, but they were losses of what was to come—becoming a mother and having a child. The loss of my mother was a loss of the past, present, *and* future. A loss of someone I had known for nearly forty-eight years. A loss of the first person I had a physical and emotional connection to, the first person I trusted. The loss of my first love.

The key to surviving the death of my mother was allowing myself to feel what I was feeling and grieving at my own pace and in my own way. When you hear someone describe mourning and grieving, they will often say that it comes in waves, which is exactly how I have experienced it. A wave will come and knock you over when you least expect it—sometimes when you are feeling your very best, your strongest, your most resilient. I used to think that I needed to immediately move away from that feeling, to overcome it, but I now understand that it is best to allow it to wash over me. Writing has helped me tremendously. I regularly write about my grief, journaling how I feel. Expressing my sorrow but also my love and gratitude for the time I had with my mother and for our beautiful bond through my creativity has given me solace.

Sometimes your gratitude will be tested. Just when you think you've mastered the cards you were dealt, you will have another hand to master—wildcards that change the very trajectory of the game. In life, we will be dealt with numerous wild cards that very well change our life and how we subsequently move forward. Yet even through these twists and turns, we still hold the power to shift our perspective. We hold the power to revere memories for what they were and to cherish and respect them.

Pause, reflect, lean in

- *Think back to a time in your life when your gratitude was tested. What happened? How did you grow?*
- *What are some memories you would like to revere and cherish from the various wildcards in your life?*

Chapter Twenty

On Reinvention of Self

I remember when the word "reinvention" would make me more than a little uncomfortable.

The word somehow evoked failure. The picture it brought to mind was of someone failing to accomplish what they set out to do and having to start "all over again." Starting over again was not what accomplished, successful people did. Starting over again was a bad thing.

Do you remember when you were growing up and you were told that you will likely change careers several times in your adult life? I seem to remember the number seven as being the number of times I would make a career change.

Whenever I heard this information, I would cringe.

Change careers repeatedly? How is that possible?

What is the point of studying something, investing all that time and money, if I am only going to change direction to something else down the road, again and again?

This cannot be accurate information. I am going to prove "them" wrong. And if this statement is somehow true, I will show "them" that I am the exception.

The last thing I wanted to do was commit to something, only to change direction down the road.

Well, I have met several people who may not have changed careers seven times but have certainly changed careers once or twice (so far) in their lifetime. And even though the "grown-up" me was not as quick to dismiss the thought that I could change careers, I still had a problem with it.

You see, when I made the decision to go to law school and graduate with a law degree, I believed that I would get a job as a lawyer and do that work indefinitely. Perhaps I would change jobs within the field of law, such as being appointed to the bench or working within the government, but I would continue working within the field of law. I would love my chosen career—the career that I had worked so hard to pursue and achieve—and I would be so passionate and driven by it that I would not even entertain the thought of doing something outside of the law.

Guess what? I did entertain thoughts of doing something else. Throughout the next two decades, I often thought about making a change. I considered returning to school to pursue my Master's in Law and applying for a position in academia so that I could teach at a law school. I thought about becoming a full-time writer, preferably fiction. I considered opening a bookstore. It's true. A fantasy of mine was to own a beautiful bookshop where authors would regularly visit and give readings. I thought about writing and operating a bookstore at the same time. But I did not act on those thoughts and ideas. I played it safe. I stayed with practicing law. It was secure, stable, interesting, and challenging work, and it was financially rewarding. Most importantly, it was consistent with the path I followed until that time. It was part of the "plan."

It was also consistent with what those around me knew I was doing and their expectations of me. It was consistent with what I defined as success. Doing something that I had planned and invested years of hard work and money undertaking. Finding the fruits of my labor and holding onto them, cultivating them, and moving along that linear trajectory.

It was all a reflection of my paradigm, the set of thoughts and beliefs that framed my behavior for many years, perhaps for my lifetime. This paradigm was rooted in several assumptions, and these assumptions had strong, stubborn roots.

First, I assumed that passion and drive meant forever. I equated doing what I loved with doing "it" for all time. Conversely, I believed that changing careers was what you did when you were unhappy with your career or, alternatively, were unsuccessful. It did not even cross my mind that you could be both happy and successful in your chosen career *and* make the decision to do something else simply because you desired to do something else!

Second, I assumed that my professional identity had to be singular. I was trained as a lawyer. I identified as a lawyer. Changing careers would entail a huge disruption to this identity—and, at the time, that was something that was an anathema to my self-awareness and under-standing. Our culture of identity "teaches" us (and this teaching truly begins in childhood) that you are *something*. It doesn't teach us that we can be *many things*. To some extent, it is a product of the education system, but it is also the product of our cultural institutions and the messaging we are bombarded with through television, film, and the media. To be fair, things have changed significantly since I was a child, and I may be generalizing to an extent. However, for the most part, we grow up believing that we must aspire to become *something*—singular.

When I was a child, I equated woman with mother. The two were interchangeable words in my early vocabulary. I assumed that a woman had babies, took care of the household, did the cooking, cleaning, and the raising of the children. I also believed that there was a smaller category of women who were "special." These were the superheroes and characters that I read about or saw on television: Charlie's Angels, Wonder Woman, and other characters of the exceptional variety. Then there were the teachers that I knew were women, but these were "my teachers," and I don't know if I actually consciously understood that these same women likely had families of their own. In my young mind, a teacher and a mother were two very separate things.

My paradigm was undoubtedly influenced by my upbringing and family circumstances. My mother was a stay-at-home mother. She did not work outside of the home (aside for a brief period of a few years when she had a part-time job). Yet my father was "Daddy," and *he* had a job. He worked outside of the home, *and* he was my daddy. As I grew older and I learned more about society and the world, I understood that you could be a mother *and* a doctor, teacher, lawyer, singer, athlete, just as a father could also be a doctor, teacher, lawyer, singer, athlete. This duality was an extremely attractive and exciting idea to me, and I fantasized about being both a mother *and* someone with a career.

What is a more recent understanding, however, is that my *professional* identity *can* be more than one thing. It may sound silly, and you may be shaking your head and wondering what planet I have been living on. It isn't that I did not understand it was possible conceptually; *I did not identify with it as something that was possible for* me. You can be a, b, and c. I can be a, b, and c. I can be a lawyer, a coach, and a writer. I can be all these things simultaneously. And being all these things does not mean that I need to actually be working in each of these roles at the same time in my life. A part of me continues to identify as a coach since resuming the practice of law. I have formal training as a coach, I am certified at two levels, and I have my certification in neurolinguistic programming (NLP). Similarly, when I was coaching, I also identified as a lawyer because I maintained my license and had a nineteen-year history practicing law. And I identify as a writer because

I love to write, I have written in various contexts in my careers as both a lawyer and a coach, and I cultivated a tremendously varied experience—one that has been further enriched as a result of coauthoring a nonfiction book and now this book.

People will attempt to fit you into boxes. Why? Because it's convenient *for them*. They will try to define *what* and *who* you are, and they will even try to keep you there, within *their* definition. They may discount your experience and skill and may criticize your new-found purpose, relegating it to the category of hobby. However, as the writer Elizabeth Gilbert so eloquently articulated in her phenomenal book *Big Magic: Creative Living Beyond Fear*:

> *"It doesn't matter in the least. Let people have their opinions. More than that—let people be in love with their opinions, just as you and I are in love with ours. But never delude yourself into believing that you require someone else's blessing (or even their comprehension) in order to make your own creative work. And always remember that people's judgments about you are none of your business."*

And further,

> "Lastly, remember what W.C. Fields had to say on this point: 'It ain't what they call you; it's what you answer to.'
> Actually, don't even bother answering.
> Just keep doing your thing."

It was only when I reread parts of Ms. Gilbert's delightful and inspirational book that I understood the meaning behind this passage. So much of what we do, who we choose to become, what parts of ourselves we choose to honor is bound to and weighted down by what we think others expect of us. It is *our* perception of what others expect *of* and *for* us, and it is rarely accurate anyway. Often, we are so caught up in trying to gain the approval of our parents, our spouse, our friends, and our peers that we fail to realize that the narrative we continue to believe about their expectations *is false*. Further, when those around us have actually expressed how they feel about our choice of career, life partner, home, life's purpose, calling, we are so fixated on what they think and how they have said it that we transform this *opinion* to fact.

Now, give this realization some careful thought. The strength of an opinion does not make it factual, much like the strength of a legal argument does not make it factual. Just because another person, perhaps someone we care about and respect and with whom we share a close relationship, expresses a thought or feeling does not make that thought or feeling true. The point is that there typically is a "backstory" to a statement that someone expresses. The context causes the person reciting the story to arrive at an opinion or to draw a conclusion. But that does not make the conclusion or opinion factual. It is merely a point of view. Feelings are not factual. Feelings are opinions, and they are subjective.

When your friend suggests that you reconsider your decision to start a business and leave your "safe and secure" biweekly paycheck-producing job, and when they express that it may be some time before you earn any income and that the business may not be sustainable, it does not mean that you will fail to earn any income for some time, nor does it mean that your business will fail.

Opinion does not equal fact.

And giving undue weight to other people's opinions is dangerous.

I am not suggesting that we should live our lives in a self-obsessed bubble without considering the diverse perspectives of those around us. That would not be pleasant or healthy. What I am suggesting is that we do not permit the opinions of others to control us and to halt our growth. When we allow that to happen, we are not living at cause, we are living in effect—we are living at the mercy of the opinions and environment around us.

What kind of a life is that?

You do not need anyone's permission to live the life that you want.

If you want to live a creative life, do it.

If you want to write novels or poetry or screenplays, do it.

If you want to write and play music, do it.

If you want to paint, draw, sculpt, do it.

If you want to work with animals, do it.

If you want to work in a profession where you are of service to others, do it.

The only permission you require is your own.

It is only when we separate who we are authentically from who we are told we are that our essence shines and we begin to live our truth.

I am a lawyer. My legal education, training, and experience have made me who I am today. During my nearly twenty-year career as a family lawyer, I have had the opportunity to learn from incredible lawyers, and this learning contributed to my becoming an excellent lawyer and shaped the professional I have become. I developed wonderful skills during my career, met amazing people, colleagues and clients, and learned so much. Every day. My entire legal experience shaped my identity. Over the years, my clients consistently praised me for helping them through the most challenging event in their lives. In my years of practice, I can count on one hand the clients with whom I had a less-than-ideal lawyer–client relationship. My clients expressed gratitude for my legal ability, my empathy and compassion, and my creativity. They praised my ability to communicate their story in a compelling manner. Through oral and written advocacy, both in a courtroom and otherwise, I told their story and advocated for their rights and entitlements. My clients expressed that hearing and seeing their story communicated gave them a voice and solidified that their story mattered.

I am also a certified coach, at the master's level, and a neurolinguistic programming (NLP) practitioner. The training I received and my experience working as a coach also shaped my identity. As a coach, I helped my clients find their voice and discover their agency to develop the confidence and skills to live intentionally and authentically and to be at cause in their lives rather than in effect, whether that was while navigating separation or divorce, infertility, or career transition. I worked with my clients to equip them to emerge from their challenge with resilience.

I am a writer and published author. When I was practicing law, I wrote extensively. During my family law career, I created compelling narratives and persuasive advocacy. For approximately ten years, I authored and edited two legal publications. In my two-year hiatus from family law, I explored and embraced my creativity in a different way. I maintained a coaching blog, I wrote for two publications, I coauthored a best-selling nonfiction book, and I wrote my memoir. I love writing. It is my passion, and I intend to do a lot more of it.

Living my best life is not just about being able to afford and enjoy luxuries such as a comfortable and attractive home, a nice wardrobe, an expensive vehicle, nice jewelry, regular vacations, and a robust bank account and investments. It is also about living from my highest, most authentic self, having a rich inner life—one that is inspired by uplifting and inspiring others—and one that is gratifying on an emotional and spiritual level. Pursuing my creativity the way that I have done over the last two years and over the last eight months, in particular, has created beautiful ripples elsewhere in my life, a gift that I did not anticipate but have wholeheartedly welcomed.

I hope that by reading my journey, you, too, have the courage to seize every moment, shine your creativity and genius brightly and boldly, and just go for it! Other people's opinions are not what will keep you fulfilled, nor will they bring you peace of mind and heart.

Whatever you choose to do, apply intentionality to it. When you reflect on the breadcrumbs, the several diverging paths that converge together to form your life path, you'll realize that nothing happens by effect alone. We have a unique path that is our own to follow for good reason. And anytime your mind and heart feel lit up with possibilities, pursue them. You never know what might come out of them. We only get one life, but when we live with intention, not only do we create our best life, but we also enjoy every minute of it—the ebbs and flows, joys and sorrows, loss and abundance.

You are multifaceted and creative (this creativity presents itself differently in each of us, but we are all creative beings). It's time to stop hiding those parts of yourself and embrace them instead. Allow yourself to shine your creativity brightly. The world needs you to show up and shine, even if they don't realize it just yet. When we step into our personal power and own every aspect of who we are, we give others around us permission to do the same. We are constantly evolving multidimensional beings, not static two-dimensional constructs. Reinventing ourselves, growing, and becoming are ways in which we live to our fullest. Our identities are composed of many intricate pieces and layers. You are not being untrue to yourself, ungrateful, or irresponsible by trying something new, shifting, and transforming your life. You are allowing yourself the freedom to unfold, which is, in my view, the most beautiful and natural thing in the world.

Pause, reflect, lean in

- *What is a desire, a possibility you have put off as a result of other people's opinions?*
- *How would it feel if you pursued this possibility once a week for an hour?*
- *What are some parts of you that have been hidden away that you still miss?*
- *What would it feel like to have those parts of yourself reemerge?*
- *What if you embraced ALL of who you are?*
- *Who would you be disappointing if you acted on these desires? Or better yet, who would you be pleasing and appeasing if you kept playing small and dimming your light? Are these individuals currently in your life? Is this individual perhaps yourself? Whoever it is, whatever it is, reclaim your power by creating a list of all the possibilities that could go right, that could work in your favor if you pursued these parts of yourself that have been hidden.*

Chapter Twenty-One

A Study of Journeys

We each have a unique journey that is unfolding within our lifetime here on Earth. We are given challenges and life events that chisel us, erode us, and sometimes uproot us from what we once knew to be true. It is a beautiful gift. While each journey is unique, resonance can be found in someone else's story through the powerful themes of strength and resilience.

THE FERTILITY JOURNEY

My fertility journey was a beautifully complex and intricate journey that made me who I am today. I am grateful for this journey, even for the difficult and painful elements of it. Though I had supportive friends and family, what was missing was another person who could resonate with what I was experiencing—the grief, the pain, the resentment, the loneliness—who could offer me empathy and sense of community and who could simply give me the space to feel what I needed to feel and to express it.

What I did not know then is that it is possible to navigate your fertility journey from a place of abundance. Infertility and abundance appear, at first blush, to be oxymorons. How can an inability to have a child have anything to do with plenty? The key to thriving through my journey was to realize that *I was enough. I* was enough, just the way that I was. *I was whole,* and even though I wanted a baby and I wanted to be a mother, I *was whole without a baby, and I was whole without being a mother.* Once I realized this truth and recognized what I did have and who I was, I felt gratitude and love for my life.

It is about fully embracing our lives, whether that looks like parenthood or not, from a place of expansion. It is about understanding and accepting that having a child a certain way and according to a specific timeline is not the goal. It is about understanding that having a biological child, conceiving a child through assisted reproduction, adopting, or not having children, does not define you or your worth as an individual or woman.

When a woman walks her fertility path from a thriving or abundance mindset, she breaks through shame, unworthiness, and lack and *embraces her full life within and beyond motherhood.* Doing so is not about abandoning the desire to become a mother. It is about making the choice of whether to continue to be attached to the desire.

When I surrendered, I released the attachment to my goal. I was no longer attached to the outcome of motherhood. I still wanted to be a mother, but I was not longing for it. This awareness is incredibly powerful. Longing kept me tied to my lack. Longing was a chronic reminder of what was missing. When I replaced longing with trust, knowing, and surrender, I became free.

When you are attached to an outcome, you are not at cause; your happiness and well-being, your joy is dependent upon an external effect—the result. I eventually developed the awareness that it should really be the reverse: the result should be dependent upon your inner state, which is, in a nutshell, the difference between living at cause and in effect.

THE SEPARATION AND DIVORCE JOURNEY

The end of a marriage or relationship is one of the most difficult events one can experience. As a family lawyer, I help my clients determine their rights and obligations arising from the demise of their relationship or marriage. I am their legal representative and advocate at perhaps the worst time in their lives.

However, as I see on the faces and hear in the words of the women and men that I represent, separation and divorce are more than legal journeys, they are life transitions involving deeply emotional, spiritual, and financial changes, as well as shifting relationships and parenting challenges. As a coach, I help people navigate this difficult path with resilience so that they are excited and empowered to step into the rest of their lives and embrace success in whatever form that takes.

I truly believe that mindset is the key to separating well; in other words, separating with clarity, confidence, and calm, with an outcome that you are at peace with, prepared to move forward with the rest of your life. I know this to be true from both my career as a family lawyer and my work as a life transition and resilience coach.

When you go through your separation from a survival mindset, you will be tethered to past events and the dominant narrative playing in your mind (and recited to your divorce professionals) will be a historical one of dependence or victimization. Operating through this lens, you will be less inclined to consider alternative ways to arrive at consensus, you will likely view every action or step taken by your former partner with suspicion, and you will make decisions and take action from emotion rather than reason. When you navigate your separation from a thriving mindset, you will be forward-thinking, be driven by reason, and will be more open to creative ways to achieving resolution. You will have a greater likelihood of not only arriving at a settlement (rather than having a court impose a decision), but you will likely get there without years of legal bills and frustration.

While the demise of a relationship or marriage is one of the most difficult life events, it can also be a journey of beautiful growth, a catalyst for transformation and a springboard toward empowerment. Beginning the work on your mindset as early as possible will prepare you for the complexities and frustrations of the family law process and empower you to move through your journey with intention, ready to wholeheartedly embrace your new beginning.

My fertility and motherhood journeys, experiencing infertility and becoming a mother at forty-two, *and* my careers as a family lawyer and resilience coach have taught me that to truly live is to *live* the journey, meaning hills, valleys, and all. If you are focusing on the destination, that point in the distant future and at the expense of the here and now, then you are truly short-changing yourself. If you relax your grip on the reins of control and trust in something a little bigger than yourself, you'll be surprised how ready and excited you will be to receive all that is within reach of your expansive embrace.

Chapter Twenty-Two

LESSONS TO LEARN AS YOU UNFOLD INTO YOUR JOY

Here are some mini coaching lessons that may help you as you navigate your own transitions along your journey called life.

THERE IS NO IDEAL OR PERFECT PARENT.

At the age of forty-two, when I believed I was a competent professional, a good lawyer, an empowered woman, I was holding a wailing baby and feeling inept and unworthy.

In the first year or so of being a mother, I constantly second-guessed myself. I was chronically worried and anxious. I was worried about my baby not receiving enough breast milk, that something must be physically or psychologically wrong with him to make him cry so much, that my son would not bond well with me in infancy, and the lack of a bond would carry over and affect his development as a child, an adolescent, and an adult.

Really.

The next moment, I would feel intense lows. These lows were different from the lows I felt during the years when my husband and I were going through infertility. I felt down, I cried easily, and I could not really understand the "source" of this sadness. When I was trying to conceive, I was sad and consciously knew that my sadness was the result of not getting pregnant. It was linked to my longing. But when I experienced sadness as a new mother, I did not consciously understand that I was sad. I just felt down, lethargic, and empty. It is only when I looked back and saw how different I began to feel when I emerged from this experience that I understood the sadness. I believe it was depression. I was never told I had depression, as I did not see my doctor about how I was feeling. I didn't even share exactly how I was feeling with anyone. But I do believe it had something to do with my perceived ineptitude as a mother, my son's nearly incessant cries, and the palpable loneliness and isolation I felt.

When I finally connected with my knowing, when I finally trusted that I was enough of a mother and I was the one who knew best—not the books I was reading, not the so-called experts in the media, not the people who were parents that I looked up to—motherhood changed from a struggle to an experience of love and peaceful connection. When

I let go of the desire to do things "perfectly," when I realized there was no such thing as "perfect," I gave myself grace, love, and permission to connect with my child through my own intuition and knowing.

YOUR RELATIONSHIP OR MARITAL STATUS DOES NOT DEFINE YOU.

You are more than the sum of you and your significant other. You are more than your relationship or marriage. While you may have been a couple for years or decades, you are a unique individual. You are not simply a wife or a husband or a partner or a spouse. You are a unique human being. And you are entitled to your own happiness, your own joy, your own purpose.

Joy is your birthright, and if your relationship is no longer a source of joy, then you are entitled to move away from it. Making the decision to leave a marriage or being told that your partner wants to leave your relationship is not something shameful. Remaining in a relationship that no longer serves you does not make you a good wife, a good parent, or a good human. Meeting the perceived expectations of others and compromising your emotional and mental health, freedom, and right to live a joyful, peaceful existence only fails one person. You.

I stayed for my children. Many people, especially women, justify their decision to remain in a marriage that is clearly not working because they have children. They fear their children will not fare well in two homes and in a family that is no longer intact. What they fail to understand is that their children *are already not faring well* and that the longer they remain in a status quo of conflict and tension, the worse they will fare. Separation and divorce do not hurt children, conflict does. Moving between two loving homes is better for children than remaining in a broken, conflict-ridden, "intact" home.

You are more important than your relationship or marriage. Embracing yourself, practicing self-compassion and self-love is more important than stoically remaining in a dynamic that is dysfunctional, hostile, abusive, or no longer joyful. You are worthy of so much more.

REINVENTION IS A REALLY GOOD THING.

Nothing stays the same. Change is one thing in life that is guaranteed. Change is a certainty.

If we try to stay the same, we inevitably fail or appear to be successful; however, this "success" comes at a price for it is an empty and hollow success that lacks joy.

Change was once my nemesis. I had a real problem with it. I was averse to it. Making a change meant that something was not working and that I had to give up. Change meant quitting.

My, how far I have come! I don't think that way anymore. Life is change. Growth is change. Staying the same is stagnation. And don't get me started on quitting. I will say this: Quitting can be very freeing, and therefore very good.

I used to think that remaining in the same job or career indefinitely was a sign of perseverance and strength. It meant that you had chosen your path wisely and excelled at it. It meant that you had accomplished what you had set out to do! But changing careers and changing jobs when you want to do so and making that choice and then following through—that is true success. I understand that now.

When I chose to stop practicing law more than two years ago to take time for myself and for my family and the challenges we were experiencing at the time, I was exhibiting perseverance, courage, and strength, as it takes all to acknowledge you need time and space to heal, to reset, to pause, and to replenish. Thereafter, when I retrained and became a coach and started my own business, I was exhibiting all those things—perseverance, courage, and strength—that I had previously believed were characteristics of someone who remained in the same career indefinitely.

When I chose to write two books that had nothing to do with law—a coauthored book of women's stories of resilience *and* a memoir, *this book*—I was exhibiting characteristics of success.

And when I resumed practicing family law while I was finalizing the manuscript to this book, I was not going back. I was unfolding into a new version of a lawyer, one with a set of new experiences and awareness and growth that came from my journey of becoming a coach and claiming my creative voice as a writer.

Learning to lean into change was not easy for me; it was definitely a process. Outgrowing who I was, my old paradigms and programming, and embracing who I wanted to be and who I was in fact becoming while trusting and knowing that I was on the right path was uncomfortable and scary at first. But it also ignited in me joy and excitement for my life.

I once thought of myself as a lawyer. Full stop. I then became a lawyer and a mother. I then unfolded into a resilience coach and a writer. Who am I today? I am all of these. Not one thing. I may be practicing family law once again, but I'm doing so from a new place with a new awareness. I am truly a multifaceted woman of many layers.

REWRITE THE STORY YOU ARE TELLING YOURSELF.

I'm not going to tell you to "think positively" because I believe that misses the mark. I'm asking you to consider the flipside of the usual story you tell yourself. I am suggesting that you turn the narrative on its head.

Growing up, I was in a perpetual state of "what if . . . negative thought, negative thought, negative thought."

I was the "what if" master.

I was the super narrator of doom and gloom and worst-case scenario.

It never occurred to me then to ask a different "what if" question. Specifically, "What if . . . good thought, good thought, good thought."

Instead of asking yourself, "What if I fail?" ask yourself, "What if I fly?"

Instead of asking yourself, "What if this doesn't work out for me?" ask yourself, "What if this works out the way it is supposed to be?"

Instead of asking yourself, "What if I hate it?" ask yourself, "What if I love it?"

The story that we tell ourselves, even a few simple words in a phrase, can affect us so powerfully. Try it out for a few days. Replace your vocabulary when you catch yourself playing the "what if" game. Play around with it and see what happens.

I think you will find that there are more reasons something will go well than will fail, that there is a greater likelihood you will find joy in a new project or endeavor, and that the worst-case scenario that you have crafted in your mind is exactly that and nothing more and that you're better off replacing it with a "joy-case scenario."

LEAN INTO YOUR GRIEF BY GIVING YOURSELF LOVE, SPACE, AND GRACE TO FEEL WHAT YOU NEED TO FEEL AT WHATEVER PACE YOU REQUIRE.

Grief is a process. It truly is. Running away from it, feeling ashamed by it, is futile. It is healthy to grieve. It is necessary to grieve.

The key to surviving the death of my mother was to allow myself to feel what I was feeling, and to allow myself to grieve at my own pace and in my own way.

I regularly expressed my grief. I did so verbally in conversation with my husband, my siblings, and our father, but I also did it through writing. For the first two or three months following my mother's death, my grief featured in my daily journaling. It was a way to unburden my mind and my soul while keeping a written record of how I was feeling, about the sadness and pain that was flowing through me. I needed to do this writing for my own sanity. There were moments when I cried so intensely that my only way to breathe was to write about it. More recently, I have expressed my grief through poetry, something that I never expected to do but somehow came to me naturally for several days. Instead of questioning it and second-guessing myself, I allowed my creativity to flow and, in the process, felt even closer to my mother.

MAKE JOY, NOT HAPPINESS, THE GOAL.

Be happy, they say.

Everyone's goal seems to be happiness. I challenge you to consider for a moment that happiness is not a worthy goal. *Joy* is.

Happiness is a state. As such, it is temporary. It is also dependent upon circumstance. It is reactive. It comes from the external, the outside.

Now, joy is something very different. Joy is not simply a state. It is much more. Joy is a way of being. It is a way of living *notwithstanding outside circumstances*. Joy is not externally dependent; it is an inside job. Being joyful comes from within. It is a way of life.

You can bring joy to any situation if you truly want to. You can bring joy to a challenge, an obstacle, a difficult event. Joy is an intentional choice. Whereas happiness is driven by an outside force, such as, for example, a new relationship, a food, a beverage, a purchase, joy is driven by one's self. To be truly joyful in life is to be a certain way at one's core.

YOU DESERVE TO UNAPOLOGETICALLY LIVE THE HIGHEST, TRUEST EXPRESSION OF YOURSELF.

Living the truest expression of yourself means leaning into your vulnerability, leaning into what makes you uncomfortable, even scared. It is about embracing all parts of you and stepping into your fullest self instead of trying to dim and hide those parts that you deem unworthy of showing and sharing. Living from your highest, truest self means abandoning shame and seeking and receiving what is rightfully yours. It is about moving forward in the face of the risk of failure. It is about moving forward *while* failing. It is about telling yourself you are worth it and that you are enough.

I *chose* the frequency I would be on, and that frequency was love and gratitude for my life, my family, my education, my career, and for all my experiences that had made me who I am and who I would become. And when I chose this higher vibration and frequency, what came back to me was fueled by that same magnetic energy, and this beautiful energy manifested in many wonderful ways.

You, too, can choose. You can choose to be at cause in your life, to stop thinking, acting, and living from a place of resistance, urgency, and fear, and to trust that what you are seeking will come to you when you are in alignment with it and when you are truly ready and open to receiving it. You can trust that you cannot get it wrong. You really can't. The choices you make and the direction your life takes are all truly for your growth. Know that your unique journey is unfolding just as it should, as long as it is in alignment with your highest self.

Allow your essence to shine. Trust in yourself to pull away from your ego—the well-intentioned but often overbearing part of you that tries to protect you and keep you within your manageable comfort zone, the zone that is free from judgment and criticism—and to rediscover your authentic, multifaceted core.

SURRENDERING IS ONE OF THE MOST POWERFUL THINGS YOU CAN DO.

I did everything I could to have a child. I tried to conceive naturally, and when that was not working, I saw a fertility specialist. I underwent IVF several times. I pursued domestic adoption.

I did all the things. I did what I thought was best. And during much of that process, I pursued my desire—to become a mother, to have a child—relentlessly and urgently.

Commitment can come at a price. It is possible to try too hard. Human beings are fascinating creatures. They have will, drive, and tenacity. And sometimes, the ego gets in the way. I wanted motherhood so badly that I was convinced I knew best. I was convinced that I would make what I wanted happen because I wanted it more than anything in the world. My ego led me down a path. I trusted my ego, and I expected that I would ultimately achieve what I wanted according to my plan.

However, the Universe had other plans for me, and it was years before I understood that. And when I finally realized it, when I finally saw it, it was incredibly freeing.

Once I had done everything I could do, I surrendered control to a power that was greater than myself. I let go of the fight, the struggle, and gave myself grace. Letting go was truly about giving myself grace and trusting in something beyond my effort.

When I surrendered, I finally felt at peace.

This surrender was not a passive act, walking away from what I desired or relenting to external forces. It was a deep and profound knowing and trust in myself and my strength, but it was also a deep and profound trust in a higher power.

This surrender was also an *active* choice to be at cause in my life, to be responsible for my life, to stop fighting against and being squeezed and molded by my circumstances, and to have an awareness and understanding that everything would evolve the way that it was meant to evolve.

This surrender was a deliberate choice to move forward, grounded in trust rather than urgency. It was a conscious decision to choose my vibration, to let go of fear, struggle, and lack, and to embrace abundance, gratitude, and love.

When I lived much of my infertility journey, I was doing so through fear. It was only when I made the decision to replace fear with love and trust, in not only myself but in a higher power, that I became free. It was only when I stopped believing that infertility was happening *to me* and asking how to make it stop, and started appreciating my life for all that it was and trusting that whatever I wanted would come to me once I was fully in alignment with it, that I found peace and felt free.

LIVE WITH AGENCY AND ACCEPT FULL RESPONSIBILITY FOR YOURSELF AND YOUR LIFE.

For some time now, I have been committed to *living at cause*. It is not easy. I slip, and I stumble regularly. But I constantly remind myself of what I need to do to remain in cause and not fall victim to living in effect.

I haven't done this work alone. While I may be a certified coach with credentials and experience, I have worked with my own coach for over a year, and I have continued a longstanding practice of educating myself and continuing my learning in this invaluable area. It is important to me, professionally and personally.

While I encourage the practice of working with a qualified coach to dive deeper into this area and to truly affect lasting change, you can make incremental shifts to help you truly become the co-creator of your life.

When I felt stuck professionally because all I thought I knew was to be a lawyer, while also feeling the pull that there was something else out there for me, my fear and need for control got in my way. When I realized that I was a multidimensional individual of many layers and started to believe in *my power to create my life*, I finally understood I could *choose* my path, one that did not have to be linear and could be whatever I desired. I have had a colorful professional journey that has led me back to practicing law and embracing it from a different and, dare I say it, enlightened perspective. This is agency, this is growth, and this is life.

Living with agency entails freedom and choice. However, it also entails responsibility. It means making the decision to be responsible for our lives, no matter what hurdles come our way. Learning about responsibility has been one of the greatest lessons from my coach and my studies and investment in my self-development and spiritual growth. I thought I understood the idea of responsibility, but I only had a superficial understanding of it. Responsibility is an amazing concept. Understanding that you are entirely responsible for your thoughts, feelings, and actions is enlightening. You can be certain that your life path will be speckled with obstacles. But you do not have to be a victim to any of these things. You can take complete responsibility for your thoughts, feelings, actions, and the results you achieve as a way to cease blaming, justifying, rationalizing. This is the way to live from your highest self. This is the way to co-create your wild and precious life.

Epilogue

I have had incredible highs and devastating lows. I have felt intense joy and equally intense sadness. I have learned to trust in my knowing, to give myself grace, and to love myself. I have learned to venture off the path to allow my intuition and creativity to guide me. I have learned to plan less and improvise more. My wild and precious life continues to unfold, and today is only the beginning.

I hope that this book has inspired and ignited your own growth and awakening. I trust that you have found resonance within its pages and that my story has empowered you to live your life a little differently, to make some small but significant shifts, to think about the ways my lessons and experiences are not that different from your own, and to apply some of the ideas explored within these pages to your own challenges and adventures. Finally, my hope is that you are no longer afraid to lean into change, that you are learning to let go and relinquish control in the face of transition, and that you are discovering and celebrating all your beautiful layers, unfolding deeper into your authentic self and joy.

Author Bio

Anita Volikis is a lawyer, author, master life coach, and NLP practitioner. Anita is passionate about how our mindset affects our ability to navigate life transitions with resilience. Anita has enjoyed a nearly two-decade–long career as a family lawyer. She currently practices family law in midtown Toronto and is committed to helping her clients separate with clarity and confidence. A prolific writer, Anita was a longstanding coauthor of *The Annotated Ontario Children's Law Reform Act* and served as associate editor of *Evidence in Family Law* for many years. Anita is a coauthor of the bestselling book *Life Love Lemonade.* She has also been featured on several podcasts and has contributed to *Thrive Global* and *Mama Brain Magazine.* She is a lover of the arts, is a voracious reader, and is a jazz enthusiast. Anita lives in Toronto with her husband, son, and golden retriever.

@anitavolikis

@anita_volikis

anitavolikis.com

Acknowledgments

Writing *Unfolding* was a phenomenal experience. It ignited emotional and spiritual growth on a level that I never quite imagined. At the end of this journey, I am left with overflowing gratitude for everyone who has played a part, directly or indirectly, in helping me transform my dream into a beautiful reality.

To the YGTMedia publishing team—Sabrina, Tania, Christine, and Doris—thank you for your skills and talents and all that you have done to help me create this incredible book. I appreciate you.

To my friends—those who have known me for close to a lifetime and those whom I met more recently—thank you for your friendship, your ear when I need it, and your love.

To my parents, Maria and John, you gave me strong roots and, more importantly, powerful and resilient wings to live my life and become the woman that I am today. I love you with all of my heart.

To my siblings, Jaimie and Steve, you are the best sister and brother anyone could ask for; I love you and thank you for your unwavering support.

Dylan, my sweet pup, you came into my life eight years ago and very recently and unexpectedly crossed that rainbow bridge. You opened up my heart allowing so much light and joy to pour inside and flow out. I will never forget you.

Jeff, you are a wonderful husband and amazing father. I can always count on you for an honest opinion of my writing, and it is appreciated more than you know. You are my steady rock and calm soul through the storms of life. I love you.

James, you are my greatest joy and blessing. Seeing you smile is everything. You make me laugh and you make me proud. I am so lucky to be your mom.

Resources and Works Cited

(in the order they appear in the book)

Oliver, Mary. "The Summer Day." *House of Light.* Beacon Press, 1990.

Monk Kidd, Sue. (@suemonkkidd) Instagram, April 13, 2021. https://www.instagram.com/suemonkkidd/

Singer, Michael A. *The Untethered Soul: The Journey Beyond Yourself.* New Harbinger, 2013.

Quotes.net, STANDS4 LLC, 2021. *"Hodding Carter Quotes."* Accessed July 12, 2021. https://www.quotes.net/quote/11661.

Benton, Robert, dir. *Kramer vs. Kramer.* Columbia Pictures, 1979.

Bridges, James, dir. *The Paper Chase.* 20th Century Fox, 1973.

Singer, Michael A. *The Untethered Soul: The Journey Beyond Yourself.* New Harbinger, 2013.

Doyle, Glennon. *Untamed.* Random House, 2020.

Delia, Lalah. *Vibrate Higher Daily.* HarperOne, 2019.

Dweck, Carol S., PhD. *Mindset: The New Psychology of Success.* Random House, 2006.

Gilbert, Elizabeth. *Big Magic: Creative Living Beyond Fear.* Penguin, 2016. (reprint)

YGTMedia Co. is a blended boutique publishing house for mission-driven humans. We help seasoned and emerging authors "birth their brain babies" through a supportive and collaborative approach. Specializing in narrative nonfiction and adult and children's empowerment books, we believe that words can change the world, and we intend to do so one book at a time.

🌐 ygtmedia.co/publishing

📷 @ygtmedia.co

f @ygtmedia.co